A BASIC GUIDE TO

Bobsledding

An Official U.S. Olympic Committee Sports Series

The U.S. Olympic Committee

Griffin Publishing Group

This Hardcover Edition Distributed By
Gareth Stevens Publishing

A World A   ompany

This hardcover edition distributed by
Gareth Stevens Publishing
A World Almanac Education Group Company
330 West Olive Street, Suite 100
Milwaukee, WI 53212 USA
Please visit our web site at: www.garethstevens.com

For a free color catalog describing Gareth Stevens' list of high-quality books and multimedia programs, call 1-800-542-2595 or fax your request to (414) 332-3567.

Library of Congress Cataloging-in-Publication Data for this hardcover edition available upon request from Gareth Stevens Publishing. Fax (414) 336-0157 for the attention of the Publishing Records Department.

Hardcover edition: ISBN 0-8368-3101-2

Editorial Statement
In the interest of brevity, the Editors have chosen to use the standard English form of address. Please be advised that this usage is not meant to suggest a restriction to, nor an endorsement of, any individual or group of individuals, either by age, gender, or athletic ability. The Editors certainly acknowledge that boys and girls, men and women, of every age and physical condition are actively involved in sports, and we encourage everyone to enjoy the sports of his or her choice.

1 2 3 4 5 6 7 8 9 06 05 04 03 02
Printed in the United States of America

ACKNOWLEDGMENTS

PUBLISHER	Griffin Publishing Group
DIR. / OPERATIONS	Robin L. Howland
PROJECT MANAGER	Bryan K. Howland
WRITER	Hans Kummer
BOOK DESIGN	m2design group
USBSF PRESIDENT	Jim Morris
EXECUTIVE DIRECTOR	Matthew Roy
MEDIA AND PUBLIC RELATIONS DIRECTOR	Julie Urbansky
EDITOR	Geoffrey M. Horn
PHOTOS AND ILLUSTRATIONS	Russ Aronheim Amy Bowyer Michael Furman Angelo Guerrera Kay Jones Chris Kraft Hans Kummer John Morgan Nancy Pierpoint Frank Posluszny Roxy Vaillancourt SKS/Seelmann U.S. Bobsled and Skeleton Federation
COVER DESIGN	m2design group
COVER PHOTO	Charlie Booker
COVER ATHLETES	Todd Hays and Pavle Jovanovic

Special thanks to Barry King of the USOC for reviewing this book and to Hans Kummer of the U.S. Bobsled and Skeleton Federation for his expertise and extraordinary help in researching, writing, and obtaining photos.

THE UNITED STATES OLYMPIC COMMITTEE

The U.S. Olympic Committee (USOC) is the custodian of the U.S. Olympic Movement and is dedicated to providing opportunities for American athletes of all ages.

The USOC, a streamlined organization of member organizations, is the moving force for support of sports in the United States that are on the program of the Olympic and/or Pan American Games, or those wishing to be included.

The USOC has been recognized by the International Olympic Committee since 1894 as the sole agency in the United States whose mission involves training, entering, and underwriting the full expenses for the United States teams in the Olympic and Pan American Games. The USOC also supports the bid of U.S. cities to host the winter and summer Olympic Games, or the winter and summer Pan American Games, and after reviewing all the candidates, votes on and may endorse one city per event as the U.S. bid city. The USOC also approves the U.S. trial sites for the Olympic and Pan American Games team selections.

Welcome to the Olympic Sports Series

We feel this unique series will encourage parents, athletes of all ages, and novices who are thinking about a sport for the first time to get involved with the challenging and rewarding world of Olympic sports.

This series of Olympic sport books covers both summer and winter sports, features Olympic history and basic sports fundamentals, and encourages family involvement. Each book includes information on how to get started in a particular sport, including equipment and clothing; rules of the game; health and fitness; basic first aid; and guidelines for spectators. Of special interest is the information on opportunities for senior citizens, volunteers, and physically challenged athletes. In addition, each book is enhanced by photographs and illustrations and a complete, easy-to-understand glossary.

Because this family-oriented series neither assumes nor requires prior knowledge of a particular sport, it can be enjoyed by all age groups. Regardless of anyone's level of sports knowledge, playing experience, or athletic ability, this official U.S. Olympic Committee Sports Series will encourage understanding and participation in sports and fitness.

The purchase of these books will assist the U.S. Olympic Team. This series supports the Olympic mission and serves importantly to enhance participation in the Olympic and Pan American Games.

United States Olympic Committee

Contents

U S A

AN ATHLETE'S CREED

The most important thing in the Olympic Games is not to win but to take part, just as the most important thing in life is not the triumph but the struggle. The essential thing is not to have conquered but to have fought well.

These famous words, commonly referred to as the Olympic Creed, were once spoken by Baron Pierre de Coubertin, founder of the modern Olympic Games. Whatever their origins, they aptly describe the theme behind each and every Olympic competition.

Metric Equivalents

Wherever possible, measurements given are those specified by the Olympic rules. Other measurements are given in metric or standard U.S. units, as appropriate. For purposes of comparison, the following rough equivalents may be used.

1 kilometer (km)	= 0.62 mile (mi)	1 mi = 1.61 km
1 meter (m)	= 3.28 feet (ft)	1 ft = 0.305 m
	= 1.09 yards (yd)	1 yd = 0.91 m
1 centimeter (cm)	= 0.39 inch (in)	1 in = 2.54 cm
	= 0.1 hand	1 hand (4 in) = 10.2 cm
1 kilogram (kg)	= 2.2 pounds (lb)	1 lb = 0.45 kg
1 milliliter (ml)	= 0.03 fluid ounce (fl oz)	1 fl oz = 29.573 ml
1 liter	= 0.26 gallons (gal)	1 gal = 3.785 liters

In Memory of
Robert "Bobby Vee" Vaillancourt
December 26, 1937–January 8, 1996
"Just Passin' Thru . . ."

Photo by Angelo Guerrera
Chassis Dynamics' Bobby Vee and Bob Cuneo trackside in Lake Placid.

About the Author...

Nancy Pierpoint

Hans Kummer is a member of the United States Bobsled and Skeleton Federation and is part of the USBSF's Bodine Project team. Hans serves as Vice President of the Federation's Connecticut Chapter. In addition, he contributes to the various branches of the USBSF, including Youth Development, as well as to the Forerunners Society, which is dedicated to preserving and relating U.S. bobsled history.

Mr. Kummer's company, Wild Child Entertainment, is developing immersive educational tools (including an IMAX film and a 3-D simulator ride as well as television and interactive projects) that explore the secrets and similarities of bobsledding and auto racing as shared through history, art, and science.

Author's Acknowledgments

So many people have influenced this book that it would be impossible to mention them all, but I would like to extend my sincerest gratitude to those people who have directly contributed.

I owe a special thanks to the USBSF Connecticut Chapter's Nancy Pierpoint (also known as The Queen and CFO) for always being a sounding board. My sincere gratitude goes to Chassis Dynamics' Bob Cuneo and Head Coach Steve Maiorca for their editorial aid. I am likewise indebted to the USBSF's Kris Alberga, Alison Flaherty, coach Tuffy Latour, and Youth Director Chris Lindsay, as well as Lisa Cox at Mattei Motorsports for assistance.

I wish to express my genuine appreciation to Albany City Historian Virginia Bowers. Ms. Bowers' exhaustive and painstaking research has provided the missing link in proving that the United States is indeed the cradle of bobsledding. I also want to thank Dr. Max Triet of the Swiss Sports Museum for providing composite information from his articles and book, *A Centenary of Bobsleighing*.

My heartfelt thanks are extended to graphic artist/designer Frank Posluszny for his outstanding artwork and photos, as well as the following contributing photographers for their generous donations: Russ Aronheim, Amy Bowyer, Chris Kraft, Michael Furman, Angelo Guerrera, Kay Jones, John Morgan, Nancy Pierpoint, Roxy Vaillancourt, and the following organizations: SKS/Seelmann-Bamberg, Germany; the Olympic Regional Development Authority; and the U.S. Bobsled and Skeleton Federation.

Introduction

**Feel the rhythm, feel the rhyme,
Get off your duff—it's bobsled time!**

So often we think there is a difference between ourselves and the athletes we watch through the media. I would simply say to you that we probably have more in common than you think.

If you have chosen to have this book in your home or classroom, you most likely have an interest in the sport of bobsledding and may even recognize the quote above, from the smash-hit Disney comedy *Cool Runnings*. Loosely based on the true story of the Jamaican Bobsled Team, the film gave broad international exposure to the sport that has been called "The Champagne of Thrills" for more than 100 years.

While it may sound like a meaningless catchphrase to some, the quote served as the motivational and unifying spirit for the athletes in the film. To feel the infectious rhythm and rhyme of U.S. bobsledding these days is nearly as thrilling as taking a ride in a sled. Anyone who is a racing fan or, for that matter, has a sense of adventure, understands. Sledding isn't just something you do; it's something you feel deep down inside yourself.

People who are not familiar with the sport may assume that bobsledding is a reckless pursuit of dangerous thrills. But the idea that bobsled athletes are merely adrenaline junkies chasing an instant fix is a fallacy. By challenging the ice, bobsled athletes look within themselves and find new depth and meaning in their abilities and thinking.

In order to survive and succeed, bobsledders must find a delicate balance between creative performance and pragmatic instinct. Very few activities require the stamina and strength to repeatedly push forward and drive 90 mph downhill on ice, sometimes pulling 6-G forces in banked turns of nearly 180 degrees. By subjecting themselves day after day to sledding's pains and joys, competitors begin to understand that life is ultimately about enduring struggle. Above all else, it is about seeking individual fulfillment or a state of grace, consequently becoming better athletes and better people.

Beyond the excitement of the sport lies the fact that bobsledding is the most expensive and technically advanced event in either the Winter or Summer Olympic Games. From the sleds themselves to the multimillion-dollar tracks, no other competition can boast of being such a true mixture of science and sport.

The U.S. Bobsled Team is riding an unprecedented wave of popularity and success after over 100 years of mainly European dominance and 40 years of not being competitive enough to win medals. This book sets the record straight and tells the complete story about America's rightful place in bobsled and Olympic history, past, present, and future.

Despite long-standing public claims by the Swiss, the organized sport of bobsledding was invented, begun, and actively pursued by Americans in the area surrounding Albany, New York. Not only did the sport begin in Albany, but as numerous publications document, including the well-known *Leslie's Weekly* (1886), the city's bobsledding events were a craze attracting literally thousands of people as spectators and participants. As was suspected for some time, America can rightfully claim the sport of bobsledding as one of only a handful of Olympic-sanctioned sports (the others include basketball, baseball, volleyball, and beach volleyball) that were first developed in the United States.

It is interesting to note that the Swiss also claim to have "engineered" the first modern bobsled, which the participants straddled rather than lying down headfirst, as they report the Americans doing with their first "sport bobsled." Contrary to these claims, the Americans had designed, built, and raced "steerable" toboggans and "straddle" sleds in Albany several years before the Swiss began to formulate their versions. A little more than 100 years later, the U.S. Bobsled Team is once again upsetting some competitors by repeatedly winning medals and breaking track records after having been relegated to second-rate status for many years. The American team's push-start was partly the result of new sled engineering and technology derived from auto racing and sponsored by NASCAR legend Geoff Bodine.

I am proud of the many friendships I have made over the years with like-minded people in the bobsled and racing communities. I cherish the unique experiences we have had together, and look forward to many more. Through these experiences, I can reflect on how much I have grown and learned. I now know more than ever the expanding value of family and the love of friendship.

There is an expression within the racing community that, in essence, states:

> **Those who *know*, understand.**
> **Those who *understand*, cannot explain.**

With that in mind, I encourage you to feel the rhythm, follow the rhyme, and become involved with the U.S. bobsled effort. Once you do, you will know and understand.

1

What Is Bobsledding?

A Brief History of Bobsledding

Sleds in one form or another have been used as a method of transportation for thousands of years. The roots of sledding as a recreational sport began in 18th-century Russia. Winter carnivals were a popular source of community spirit in St. Petersburg. In 1750, at a carnival, a Russian showman introduced the construction of wood-framed ice slides for sledding.

Catherine the Great, empress of Russia, possessed a thirst for adventure. She was a frequent participant on the ice slides and declared that it was one of her favorite activities. She even offered suggestions for improving the ride.

In 1804 a Frenchman returned to Paris after being intrigued by the popularity of the wooden ice slides he saw in St. Petersburg. Inspired to create a slide better suited to the weather in Paris, he built a large wooden hill with tracks instead of ice, and designed a vehicle with wheels rather than sled runners to roll down the incline. In the process, he created the world's first roller coaster. In honor of the earliest Russian ice slides, this first version of the roller coaster was dubbed "The Russian Mountains." In fact, in some countries, roller coasters are known as "Russian Mountains" to this day.

The sport of competitive sledding, however, didn't begin until the late 19th century, when bobsledding clubs of lumberjacks in Albany, New York, first raced against each other on sleds they used to haul wood. As many as 30 men would straddle an individual sled at race time. Steering wheels were mounted to both sets of front and back runners. The earliest sleds had no brakes. A speeding sled was usually stopped with the aid of a garden rake, which slowed the sled down enough to allow the riders to drag their feet without getting hurt.

As early as 1882, the Albany Bobbing (Coasting) Association was organized to oversee the many clubs that were forming. The clubs were no longer confined to lumberjacks and were open to anyone capable of putting together a sled and team. The Association held races, parades, and winter carnivals on a regular basis. These events were attended by thousands of people (one

Leslie's Weekly, January 30, 1886

The bobsled craze hits Albany.

unofficial newspaper tally indicated 50,000 participants), which is an amazing feat given the lack of modern transportation and media exposure.

The first racing sleds were made of wood, but steel sleds would soon replace them. Newspaper articles from 1886 indicate that significant improvements in construction were made that year. Simple wooden planks gave way to "fancy paint, gold lettering, cushions and ... complicated steering apparatus [along with] lantern headlights and steel brakes."

In the winter of 1888–89, Albany resident Stephen Whitney, an avid bobsledder and the secretary/treasurer of the Albany Gas Company, traveled to Davos, Switzerland, as part of a European Grand Tour honeymoon following his second marriage. After seeing the Swiss race toboggans, he introduced the sport of bobsleigh to the public at the popular winter resort. The winter of 1889–90 saw the first steel sled with rope steering debut in Switzerland, possibly racing down the slope from St. Moritz to Celerina. The sled, developed by a Major Bulpett and Christian Mathis, was a two-seater or multi-seater, which the team straddled.

St. Moritz, Switzerland, quickly followed Davos's lead and added the sport to its roster of recreational activities. The winners' list at the first St. Moritz races indicates that there were no fixed categories: three-man to six-man teams were judged equally. The thrilling sport quickly took off and became popular at many other resorts. By 1911 there were about 60 runs in Switzerland. Soon Germany, Austria, Romania, and Silesia (now Poland) also followed suit, opening new runs nearly every year in some of the remotest valleys. Even Germany's Crown Prince Wilhelm was an ardent bobsledder.

It is important to remember that most of these runs were no more than ordinary streets or forest paths with snow-reinforced curves. Crowd and pedestrian safety was a constant concern. By 1914, sled races were taking place on a wide variety of natural ice courses.

What originated as a sport among middle-class people now was largely becoming an activity for the rich and adventurous, who gathered at Alpine resorts for weekends of competition and parties. Participant training did not exist at the time. Competitors simply got together and bought or rented a sled. A bobsledder might start as a rider and then take the wheel after a few trial runs.

In 1923 the Fédération Internationale de Bobsleigh et de Tobogganing (FIBT) was founded to govern the sport worldwide. The following year a four-man race took place at the first-ever Winter Olympics in Chamonix, France. A two-man event was added at the 1932 Olympics in Lake Placid, New York. Ever since then, the format of running both four-man and two-man races in the Winter Olympics has been used.

In the 1950s the sport as we know it today began to take shape. The streamlined shape of automobiles and aircraft developed during the 1930s and '40s began to inspire the body design of the modern bobsled. The critical importance of the start was recognized, as strong and fast athletes in other sports were drawn to bobsledding. Track and field competitors, football players, gymnasts, and others who could deliver an aggressive push were actively sought. A critical rule change in 1952, however, ended the era of the super heavyweight bobsledder. The ruling limited the total weight of the crew and sled, ensuring that the sport would attract the best athletes, not just the biggest. As sled and track technology advanced, so too did the athletic ability and training of the crews. Today, the world's top teams train year-round and compete mostly on artificial ice tracks in sleek high-tech fiberglass and steel sleds.

Until the creation of the World Cup competition in the mid-1980s, bobsled success was solely determined by performance at the Olympics and the World and European Championships. Since its debut, however, the World Cup series has added an exciting new dimension to the sport, in which versatility on different tracks and season-long consistency are valued and rewarded.

Over the years, bobsledding has been largely dominated by Europe's Alpine nations. By far the most successful nations have been Switzerland and Germany. The Swiss have won more medals in Olympic, World, and European championships than any other country. East Germany emerged as the sport's major power in the mid-1970s with its emphasis on sled design and construction. Since their country's reunification, the German bobsledders have remained a formidable group, winning numerous Olympic medals and World Championship titles since 1990. The Swiss and Germans have also won the most World Cup competition medals, followed closely by Canadian teams.

The British won numerous medals during the sport's adolescence in the 1930s, '40s, and '60s, and then again in the '90s. Italy has a long and successful track record in the sport, particularly from the mid-'50s to the late '60s, and Austria has continued to have its shining moments. From the small core of Alpine nations that originally embraced bobsledding, the sport has been expanding around the world to include countries such as Jamaica, Japan, Australia, and New Zealand. Nagano, Japan, was the host for the 1998 Winter Olympics and has built one of the world's newest and fastest artificial ice tracks.

Although the traditional bobsled powers remain strong, other nations have begun to show their strength. The 1995–96 World Championships in Winterberg, Germany, saw no fewer than eight nations place in the top ten in the four-man event, while seven nations were represented in the two-man top ten finishes.

The U.S. bobsled community can now draw on a rich history as it charts the course to a promising future. The United States has always been a nation of firsts, and the sport of bobsledding is no exception. In addition to the fact that the United States invented the sport and nurtured it in its infancy, America was a consistently strong presence in bobsledding competition from 1928 to 1956. Recently, U.S. competitors have unveiled new sled technology and athlete training programs and, consequently, have been winning runs and shattering track records. This resurgence follows 40 years

Nancy Pierpoint

International athletes and officials in the sled area at St. Moritz

of mediocre performances and habitual mockery by fellow competitors. In fact, the United States has not won an Olympic medal of any color in bobsledding since 1956.

Another stage in the sport's evolution came in the early 1990s when the United States was one of the first nations to debut a women's bobsled team at events in North America and Europe.

One of the newest and most modern artificial ice tracks in the world had its 1997 premiere in Park City, Utah. This track was designated as a focal point for the 2002 Olympic Winter Games in Salt Lake City. New York State financed the construction of a new state-of-the-art track for bobsled, luge, and skeleton in Lake Placid, New York, to replace the old facility, which hosted the 1932 and 1980 Winter Olympics. The 20-turn track was completed in February 2000, just in time to host the inaugural Winter Goodwill Games. The new facility in Lake Placid has been awarded the 2003 Men's Bobsled World Championships. With the national bobsledding program established, youth and athlete recruitment programs in place, and the sport's popularity on the rise, there has never been a better time for Americans to become involved.

Why Is It Called Bobsledding?

There are a couple of theories as to the origin of the name *bobsled*. The most popular and plausible explanation is that the name arose as an attempt to differentiate a single toboggan from a vehicle that consists of two sleds (front and rear) joined together.

The use of the term *bobsled* is found as early as the 1830s in the United States. At that time, a bobsled, employed by lumberjacks for the main purpose of transporting timber, consisted of two individual toboggan-type sleds connected to each other. Early writers refer to a *pair of bobs* and seem to distinguish between a front and rear bob. The joining of the two bobs presumably gave the vehicle greater mobility and maneuverability along narrow forest paths.

The use of the term *bob* to mean a hanging or dangling object has a long history in English. It's reasonable to assume, therefore, that *bobsled* originally referred to the second sled hanging, like a bob, from the first. By way of analogy, the term *bob* later meant the first sled and over time was applied to the whole vehicle.

In English, the verb *to bob* can also mean "to move quickly up and down." This reference has led some people to believe the name came from the fact that early bobsled riders would work together to increase a sled's speed in the straightaways. The participants slowly leaned back and then quickly "bobbed" into an upright position, giving the sled greater forward motion.

The origin of the word *sled* is fairly easy to deduce. The Middle Dutch term *slede* made its way into England in the 14th century and became *sledge*. This word was taken to the United States by English settlers and was later replaced by *sleigh*. The latter is a linguistic variant on the Dutch *slee* and was introduced into American English by 18th-century Dutch settlement along the Hudson River.

What Is a Bobsled Race?

Bobsled teams include a brakeman and a pilot in the two-man event; two crewman/pushers are added for the four-man race. From a standing start, the crew pushes the sled in unison for up to 50 meters. This distance is typically covered in less than six seconds, and speeds of 25 mph are reached before the crew loads into the sled.

Although the difference in start times among the top crews is measured in tenths or even hundredths of a second, a fast start is critical. As a rule of thumb, a one-tenth of a second lead at the start translates into a three-tenths of a second advantage by the bottom of the course. Once the team has loaded into the sled, the main responsibility becomes that of the driver, who must pick the fastest lines to drive into and out of each turn. The rest of the crew is crouched down in a tuck position behind the driver to maximize aerodynamic airflow over and around the sled.

During a typical 60-second run, speeds in excess of 80 mph are reached, and crews are subjected to a force of more than four times gravity (more than 4 G's, or over four times body weight). By comparison, astronauts aboard the space shuttle feel only a 3-G force upon launch.

The World Cup Circuit

World Cup competitions are awarded by the FIBT to member countries through a bidding process. Competitions may be awarded either to a country or to a specific track within a country. Each country is allowed to race one sled per event. Additional sleds must make a qualifying run.

In World Cup competition, two heats (runs) are conducted during the course of one day for each event. At the Olympics and World Championships, four heats are held over two days in both the two-man and four-man events. Unlike men's bobsled, the women's team only races two heats over one day of competition during the Olympic Games and the World Championships. The crew with the lowest combined time is the winner.

The Starting Order

A seeding system determines the start positions at all major bobsledding events. Since the ice becomes rougher as the competition progresses, it is an advantage to be among the first sleds on the track. The seeding system rewards the top crews (based on previous results) with the best start positions. Similarly, the rest of the field is seeded in additional groups based on previous results.

At the first World Cup competition of each season, the final results from the previous season apply. Places 1 to 10 are allocated on the basis of World Cup results. For the remainder of the season, starting groups are based on current World Cup results, as follows:

- Group I—1 to 10
- Group II—11 to 20
- Group III—21 to 30
- Group IV—31 and above.

Team Ranking

In each World Cup race, points are awarded to the top 30 finishers in men's bobsled and to the top 25 finishers in women's bobsled. In men's bobsled, World Cup titles in the two-man, four-man, and overall events are won by teams accumulating the most points over the season. Women's bobsled teams are awarded a two-member season title.

What Is a Bobsled Track?

Today, the bobrun in St. Moritz, Switzerland, is the only natural ice track left that holds certified races. Each year, the track's length and depth are carved out of the ice and snow to follow the natural contour of the St. Moritz terrain.

Most competition now takes place on tracks made of a concrete base, with an artificial ice surface supplied by a plumbing system installed alongside the track. Most venues are located on the north side of a slope, to take advantage of proper sunlight conditions. All tracks have uniform lighting, athlete warmup areas, bobsled work areas, first-aid and press centers, transportation and communications facilities, and start and finish buildings, as well as solar/weather covering to protect sensitive areas of the track from damage.

Nancy Pierpoint

A four-man Bo-Dyn as it slingshots through the
natural curves at St. Moritz, Switzerland

The standard length of a track is approximately 1,500 meters (nearly one mile), sloping downhill. All courses drop a minimum specified vertical distance and feature numerous banked curves from top to bottom. Each track has unique characteristics and includes elements of varying technical difficulty. The elements that place the greatest demands on driving technique are usually located in the first stretch, which accounts for two-thirds of the track.

The Starting Area

This bobsled push-off stretch is at the top of the track and is defined as the 50-meter area between the starting block and the first set of electric timing eyes. It includes a frozen base wide enough to accommodate two sleds (one racing, one in preparation) and two grooves in the ice base in front of the block to give the sled runners a guide path upon starting. Once the athletes and sled have broken the light beam between the timing eyes, the race clock is automatically activated.

Curves

Bends in the track are constructed in such a way as to provide a band of possible trajectories from which a driver may choose. In the central part of a turn, the trajectory extends along the upper half of the curve. Entries and exits from turns are rounded so that the sleds can take them smoothly without risk of flipping over, provided no mistakes are made in driving.

Guardrails and lips are also constructed to help return the

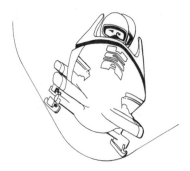

Illus. by Frank Posluszny

sled to the track, should the sled go too high. A 4-G centrifugal force on a team lasts for a maximum of three seconds. A 5-G centrifugal force is maximum in competition and lasts no longer than two seconds.

Straights

These sections allow a sled to pick up speed, provided the driver has chosen an appropriate trajectory coming out of a turn. The straight, also known as a chute, provides a transition stretch for the sled so that it is in a correct alignment going into another turn. The section of track where a bend links into a straight gradually runs into the straight's side wall, so that the sled does not meet an abrupt change in angle. The height of a side wall in an iced straight typically is 12 feet. As a sled nears the end of the run, it passes a second set of electric timing eyes at the finish line that stops the clock. The sled then enters the deceleration stretch, which is a gradual ascent to slow the sled down. It is at this point that the brakeman in the sled leans down and pulls on the brake lever to cut the speed still further. Some tracks also have a post or finish curve that further decelerates the sled, but this can pose a problem to teams that are trying to maintain control of the sled.

International Bobsled Tracks

A wide variety of terrain configurations poses a continual challenge for a bobsled team, particularly the driver, to master. It is recommended that competitors further review FIBT layouts of the tracks to familiarize themselves with the technical difficulties of each venue. There are 12 bobsled runs in the world, predominantly in Europe:

Austria
  Igls

Canada
  Calgary

France
  La Plagne

Germany
  Altenberg
  Königssee
  Winterberg

Italy
  Cortina d'Ampezzo

Japan
  Nagano

Norway
  Lillehammer

Switzerland
  St. Moritz

United States
  Lake Placid, NY
  Park City, UT

The Two U.S. Bobsled Tracks

Mount Van Hoevenberg, Lake Placid, New York, now hosts the old and new of bobsledding in the United States. The old track dates back to 1930, when the mountain was selected as the site of the 1932 Olympic bobsled competition. Originally a 1.55-mile track, the bobrun was shortened in the mid-1930s to a 16-curve, 1-mile track, and then again in 1989 to a 16-curve, 1,400-meter track.

The original bobsled run was cut into Mt. Van Hoevenberg's side. The bobrun consisted of earthen straightaways and stone-faced curves. In later years, for safety reasons, lips were added to the curves and wooden sides to the straightaways. In the late 1960s the finish curve was refrigerated.

After the 1980 Winter Olympics was awarded to Lake Placid, the bobrun was completely rebuilt, copying the original design. Refrigeration was extended along the entire length, with 33 miles of pipe buried in the 2,000 cubic yards of concrete. With the completion of the refrigerated run in 1979 came the added bonus of an extended season from early December to early March. Today, the track suffers from an antiquated refrigeration system and outdated design. Because of these problems, and because renovation funds are limited, the bobrun is not certifiable for international four-man competition. The track has hosted the 1949, 1961, 1969, 1973, 1978, and 1983 World Championships.

A new combined bobsled/luge/skeleton track at Mt. Van Hoevenberg was completed in February 2000. The 20-turn, 1,455-meter track proved taxing for many of the two-man sleds during the Winter Goodwill Games. Of the ten sleds in the competition, only five finished, with Sandis Prusis and Janis Ozols of Latvia winning the gold medal. Americans Brian Shimer and Pavle Jovanovic won the bronze. Following the Goodwill Games, changes were made to the facility, including modifying the outlets of a few turns, perfecting the ice, and raising some lips throughout the track. Subsequently, the new track hosted the 2001 Men's Bobsled World Cup Finale. Americans Todd Hays, Pavle Jovanovic, Randy Jones, and Garrett Hines won the contest, earning the United States its first gold medal since 1997.

Utah Olympic Park, Park City, Utah, is one of the world's newest and most athletically challenging bobsled tracks. This state-of-the-art facility, which debuted in 1997, features the fastest speeds of any artificially iced track. Built as a cost of $25 million, the track is 1,340 meters long, with 15 curves. Its vertical drop is 390 feet, and the average run time 48 seconds at approximately 81 mph.

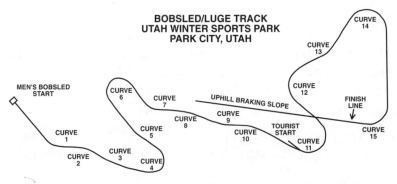

Illustration by Frank A. Posluszny

The track is served by a 1,216-ton ammonia refrigeration plant, with a refrigeration capacity of 13,000 tons. The plant pumps liquid ammonia through more than 60 miles of evaporator refrigeration tubing embedded in 72,000 square feet of shotcrete surface supported by 86 miles of reinforcing steel.

This bobrun has been designated to serve as the bobsledding competition venue for the 2002 Winter Olympic Games in Salt Lake City. It will also be a primary World Cup competition and athletic training site, as well as part of Salt Lake City's Community Olympic Development Center, in conjunction with the USOC and the USBSF.

Track Facts

Nagano, Japan, played host to the 1998 Olympic Winter Games. The bobsled track at Mount Iizuna is one of the newest bobruns in the world. Bobsledders have nicknamed it "The Spiral." The track is more than three-fourths of a mile long and follows the natural terrain with 15 jolting twists and turns. It also has something no other bobsled track in the world has: two *uphill* sections as part of the actual racecourse. Any mistake made by a team during a run on this track can prove costly, as the sled may lose the speed needed to power up the slope.

While it was part of Yugoslavia, Sarajevo played host to the 1984 Olympic Winter Games. In 1984, Sarajevo was a unique point of convergence for the world, as representatives of East and West, Communism and Capitalism, Islam and Christianity all met to celebrate each other's common humanity. The 1990s brought brutal destruction and savage killing to the region, as Serbs, Muslims, and Croats fought for control of the city and surrounding areas of Bosnia-Herzegovina.

The bobsled run on Mount Trebevic, overlooking the city center, now has basketball-sized holes from the artillery that shelled the city from 1992 to 1995. Cable cars that once took visitors to the top are now bashed and scattered on the rocky slope. The walls of the hilltop restaurant are pierced with bullet holes from the execution of war prisoners. While tensions have not been completely resolved, an international campaign is under way to rebuild the city and its Olympic venues, with the hope of winning the bid to host the 2010 or 2014 Winter Olympic Games.

What Is the FIBT?

The Fédération Internationale de Bobsleigh et de Tobogganing (FIBT) is the international governing body for bobsled and skeleton. It comprises all 48 countries that have national governing bodies responsible for amateur bobsledding and skeleton and that agree to abide by the rules and provisions as set by the FIBT.

Founded in 1923, the FIBT is based in Milan, Italy, and is led by a World Congress and an Executive Committee, which supervises all activities relating to bobsledding and skeleton. The FIBT establishes the rules for the two sports and controls all World Championships and Continental Championships as well as participation in the Olympic Games. The organization ensures the existence of proper conditions for safe performance at international competitions. It also actively promotes amateur bobsledding and skeleton as competition sports to the general public.

What Is the USBSF?

The United States Bobsled and Skeleton Federation (USBSF) is the national governing body for the United States in the international amateur sports of bobsledding and skeleton. The USBSF is a nonprofit corporation that was formed to advance, encourage, improve, and promote amateur competition in the United States. The Federation is recognized by the FIBT, the U.S. Olympic Committee (USOC), and the International Olympic Committee (IOC) to represent the United States.

Among other administrative functions, the USBSF is responsible for submitting to the USOC the criteria and procedures to be followed by the United States in the sports of bobsled and skeleton for each Olympic Games. The USBSF is governed by a Board of Directors and a staff at the national office in Lake Placid, New York.

As the primary coordinating organization for bobsledding and skeleton in the United States, the USBSF works to create national and grassroots interest and participation in these sports. The USBSF has approximately 500 members, including athletes of all ages, coaches, officials, parents, and fans who are working together to strengthen the sports. The organization is responsible for the selection and training of teams to represent the United States in international competition. It also conducts national races and championships, and holds national training camps and recruitment events for athletes. The USBSF supports various clubs of sliders in all age groups throughout the country.

What Is the Sport of Skeleton?

Sliding headfirst, with face down and hands back, skeleton athletes race down the icy bobsled tracks of the world at speeds approaching 80 mph. Technically, skeleton is the world's oldest sliding pastime. The sport was largely organized in the late 1800s in the village of St. Moritz, Switzerland. The races had men and women descending the Cresta Run, the icy slope from St. Moritz to the town of Celerina. The winner received a bottle of champagne.

Skeleton appeared in the 1928 and 1948 Olympic Games at St. Moritz; an American won the gold medal in 1928. The sport faded from popularity until the late 1970s, when a resurgence started in Europe. Since then, more than 20 nations have joined the ranks, participating in World Cup and World Championships held annually. Beginning in October in Calgary, Alberta, Canada, and December in Lake Placid, New York, competition can be witnessed weekly.

The skeleton sled is 3 feet long and 16 inches wide, weighing from 70 to 115 pounds, depending on the slider's body weight. The sleds are made of steel or fiberglass. The bottom of the sled is a flat steel pan on which the slider's nation, start number, and sponsors appear.

The slider wears a helmet with a chin guard because the athlete's face is a mere two inches from the ice. A slider uses sprinter's spikes, and a skintight rubber suit is worn to increase aerodynamics. Like bobsledders, skeleton sliders use a quick 50-meter sprint to start their sleds at the top of the track. Loading is accomplished by a smooth lunge onto the sled. At speeds of 70 to 80 mph, the athlete negotiates the curved track using subtle shifts in body weight and positioning.

Nancy Pierpoint

FIBT Materials Commissioner Bob Cuneo with monument at the birthplace of skeleton in St. Moritz, Switzerland

The International Olympic Committee announced in October 1999 that skeleton would be added as a full medal event at the 2002 Winter Olympic Games. The U.S. men's and women's skeleton teams finished in the top two in the world during the 2000–01 season.

2

U.S. Bobsled Teams

The U.S. Bobsled Team competes on the world circuit, commencing in late October and ending in mid-March. The addition of the Park City facility and the new combined track in Lake Placid offers the team more accessible and effective training and a "home field" advantage in future competitions.

The U.S. Bobsled Team is one of the few national teams not funded by its government. The U.S. athletes are not paid for their time during their training season, either. This poses a major disadvantage for the United States, as the USBSF can keep the athletes on a consistent training schedule for only five months a year. During the off-season, athletes are forced to find temporary work or go on individual fundraising campaigns to keep themselves financially afloat. Other dominant world teams typically have the financial ability to remain together during that time. This gives them an advantage in training, filling sponsorship requirements, building and maintaining advanced equipment, and mentally preparing themselves for competition. With a comparable level of support, the U.S. team could inevitably achieve greater and more consistent competitive dominance.

Contrary to popular belief, the U.S. team is not funded by tax dollars. National and global sponsors of the Olympic Games fund the USOC. The funds are distributed by the USOC to the governing bodies for amateur sports in the United States. The amount that the U.S. Bobsled Team receives accounts for one-third of the funding needed to compete on the world circuit.

The rest of the money needed to cover competition expenses must come from corporate and individual sponsors and donations. The USBSF has garnered support from official corporate sponsors and suppliers such as AIT Worldwide Logistics; Adidas; Holme, Roberts & Owen; HK Systems; American Skandia; Auto Europe; Duofold; Milestones Mall; and Sports and Sponsorships. Other revenue sources for the USBSF include profits gained from the sale of its merchandise and fundraising efforts such as auctions and dinners.

Competitive Challenges

The U.S. Bobsled Team faces many of the same challenges that a NASCAR (National Association for Stock Car Automobile Racing) team has in keeping a competitive race car on the track.

- After research and development, custom design and assembly, a competition bobsled costs $100,000 to design (and as much as $35,000 to build each sled thereafter) and $10,000 to maintain each season. The U.S. men's team travels with six sleds (three two-man and three four-man sleds) and the women's team travels with three two-woman sleds.
- Depending on shape and alloy composition, a set of sled runners will only be fast in certain conditions and on certain tracks—just like a car's tires. A fast set of runners costs $5,000, and a competitive team should have several sets.
- The U.S. Bobsled Team needs to assemble and employ a technical team similar to the pit crew of a NASCAR team to build, maintain, prepare, and repair its equipment.
- The U.S. Men's Bobsled Team transports 10,000 pounds of equipment and 13 athletes (three drivers plus three push athletes to fill out each four-man team, as well as one alternate push athlete), three coaches, and four technical staff across

the Atlantic Ocean four times a year for the World Cup and World Championship seasons. The women's team transports 10,000 pounds of equipment, six to eight athletes, and three coaches between Europe and North America three to four times a year.

- While on tour, the team must rent three vans, two trucks, and two trailers. At each venue, it must set up a workshop, house and feed the athletes and staff, rent practice time on the ice, and videotape each bobsled driver's trajectory lines through every corner of a 15- or 16-curve track.

Despite these challenges, the U.S. Bobsled Team is committed to push-starting the future.

U.S. Bobsledding—The Early Years

Aside from being the cradle of bobsledding in the late 19th century, the United States has had many defining moments in the history of the sport.

1928—A five-man U.S. team, driven by 17-year-old Billy Fiske, won an Olympic gold medal at St. Moritz, Switzerland. An American sled driven by Jennison Heaton also won the silver medal. The only occasion when five-man competition was held in the Olympics was in 1928.

Fiske is regarded as a pioneer of U.S. bobsledding. Three of his team members (Nion Tucker, Geoffrey Mason, and Richard Parke) had never seen a bobsled before and were chosen after answering an ad in the Paris edition of the *New York Herald Tribune*. It was Mason's first and last ride in international bobsled competition.

Fiske would later achieve the tragic distinction of being the first American pilot killed in World War II. He joined England's Royal Air Force in 1939 and was killed in 1940 at the age of 29 while flying his Hurricane fighter plane in the Battle of Britain over southern England.

1932—A bobrun facility with 26 curves at Mt. Van Hoevenberg in Lake Placid, New York, was commissioned to host the competition during the 1932 Olympic Games. This competition also featured the first Olympic-sanctioned two-man bobsled race. The weather was so poor during the Games that the four-man bob races had to be postponed until after the official closing ceremony.

Lake Placid residents J. Hubert Stevens, 41, and his brother Curtis, 33, won the gold in two-man. They were convinced that their success was due, in part, to the fact that they heated the sled runners with blowtorches for 25 minutes. Considered unusual but acceptable at the time, this practice soon became illegal.

Billy Fiske captured his second gold medal, as driver of the four-man team. His main rival was the Saranac Lake Red Devils team driven by civil engineer Henry Homburger, who won the silver in four-man competition.

Fiske's four-man rider Eddie Eagan had won an Olympic gold medal in 1920 as a light heavyweight boxer. Coming from a poor family in Denver, Eagan made his way through Yale, Harvard Law School, and Oxford to become a successful lawyer married to an heiress. He later won the U.S. amateur heavyweight title and became the first American to win the British amateur championship. Fiske and Eagan's other teammates included 48-year-old Jay O'Brien, who was head of the U.S. Olympic Bobsled Committee, and 40-year-old "Tippy" Gray, an accomplished songwriter. Gray was such a modest man that his children never knew that he had won two Olympic gold medals until after he died in 1941. Eagan was the only team member to survive World War II. He died in 1967 and was buried with both of his gold medals.

1936—The United States won Olympic gold and bronze in two-man competition in Garmisch-Partenkirchen, Germany. Gold-winning driver Ivan Brown of Keene Valley, New York, was perhaps the most superstitious of all bobsledders. For luck, he needed to find at least one hairpin on the ground each day. As luck would have it, he was able to complete the task for 24 consecutive days preceding the Olympics. Brown was also the only driver to race without goggles: he claimed that they added wind resistance and dulled his eyesight.

J. Hubert Stevens and his team placed fourth in the four-man competition. Up-and-coming driver Francis "Art" Tyler finished sixth in the four-man.

1948—Following the end of World War II, the United States struck Olympic gold in the four-man championship and bronze in the

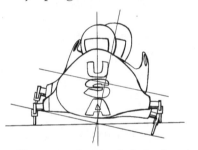

Illustration by Frank A. Posluszny

two-man competition in St. Moritz. Winning gold in the driver's seat of the four-man was Art Tyler, a Kodak engineer who designed, built, and raced his own sleds—the first sleds to use an articulated front and back (meaning that each could rotate independently from side to side).

1952—For the first time since it began competing in Olympic bobsledding, the United States failed to win a gold medal. However, the team did manage to garner silver behind Germany in both competitions in Oslo, Norway.

1956—The final Olympic medal in the 20th century for U.S. bobsledders came this year in Cortina d'Ampezzo, Italy, when Art Tyler's team won the bronze medal in the four-man race. Team USA placed fifth and sixth in two-man competition, with Art Tyler driving the sixth-place sled.

1960—A low point in U.S. bobsled history came this year when Squaw Valley, California, hosted the Olympic Games. The Squaw Valley promoters were disgusted with the cost of building and operating a bobrun and declined to build one. Young people who might have been attracted to the sport went elsewhere, leaving American interest strictly limited to the Lake Placid area. As a result, the Morgan family's Dew Drop Inn in Lake Placid became the unofficial headquarters of U.S. bobsledding.

The spirit of sledding, including its tragedies and triumphs, has been a Morgan family calling for several generations. Jim Morgan, son of team manager Forrest Morgan, was designated as the driver for both No. 1 sleds in the 1976 two-man and four-man Olympic competition in Innsbruck, Austria. The team finished a disappointing 14th in the two-man and 15th in the four-man.

1964—The United States finished fifth in two-man competition and sixth in four-man at the 1964 Innsbruck Olympics.

1968—U.S. bobsledders placed sixth in the two-man bob in the Olympics at Grenoble-Alpe d'Huez, France.

1980—Lake Placid once again hosted the Winter Olympics. The U.S. Bobsled Team finished fifth and sixth in the two-man bob. Emerging athletes Brent Rushlaw and Joseph Tyler were credited with the sixth-place finish. American bobsledders Willie Davenport and Jeffrey Gadley, who finished 12th, are believed to be two of the first black athletes to compete in the Winter Olympics.

1984—The Winter Olympics in Sarajevo once again saw the American bobsledders place fifth in the four-man competition.

1988—The Winter Olympics in Calgary saw Brent Rushlaw's four-man team race clean heats but ultimately take fourth place, just two one-hundredths of a second behind the bronze medal.

1992—The Olympics in Albertville, France, looked hopeful with powerhouse athlete Brian Shimer and National Football League superstar Herschel Walker on the same team. Unfortunately, team dynamics and preparation did not live up to the media hype, and the team finished seventh in the two-man bob.

Kay Jones

The Morgan brothers (driver Jim, Sean #2, Bryan #3, brakeman John) crash during the 1980 Olympic Trials on Lake Placid's "Zig and Zag corner" (the bobrun's most difficult turn).

The Bodine Connection

The tide began to turn for U.S. bobsledders in 1992, but in an unexpected way. NASCAR driving legend Geoff Bodine saw the team's poor performance. He immediately realized that race car drivers and bobsledders had much in common.

Geoff's career highlights include 1994 Winston Select and Busch Pole Awards, 1992 Busch Clash Winner, 1987 IROC Champion, 1986 Daytona 500 Champion, and 1982 NASCAR Winston Cup Rookie of the Year. In addition to introducing modern power steering and full-face helmets to NASCAR Winston Cup racing, Geoff holds the *Guinness Book of World Records* listing for the most wins (55 modified races) in one season. His Winston Cup career totals include more than 500 races, 18 wins, nearly 40 poles, close to 100 top-five finishes, and nearly 200 top tens, as well as more than $14 million in winnings. In 1997, he made modern racing history when he won the Atlanta NAPA 500 Pole with a track record speed of 197.478 mph—the fastest qualifying lap ever at a Winston Cup track other than Daytona or Talladega.

The Bodine family name has become synonymous with all types of racing. All three Bodine brothers—Geoff, Brett, and Todd—have competed in the NASCAR Winston Cup Series.

After some preliminary investigation about bobsledding, Geoff Bodine flew to Lake Placid and test-drove a sled, damaging it in the process. Steering a bobsled is not as easy as it might look. After taking the ride, he commended the athletes who had mastered the sport using such old and outdated equipment. He definitely felt much more at ease in the safety of his new stock car. However, Geoff's thoughts about the similarities between the two sports were confirmed. Many of the qualities that make a good race car driver are shared by bobsledders, including being

Chris Kraft

NASCAR legend Geoff Bodine

able to drive the proper line into and out of a turn, as well as the physical training needed to withstand intense G forces and accomplish tasks with precision timing.

Two problems existed, however. First, the bobsledders did not have a sustained year-round training program to help them prepare for competition. Second, and more important, the U.S. athletes were using inferior, secondhand equipment purchased from European competitors. No wonder the United States was doing so poorly in the sport! There wasn't much that Geoff Bodine could do about the first problem other than make suggestions, but he could definitely help solve the second problem.

Shortly after his Lake Placid trip, Bodine founded the USA Bobsled Project for the sole purpose of funding research, development, and manufacturing of American equipment for American athletes. The plan: Apply high-tech race car design and construction technology to build a faster, lighter bobsled. The advantage of having a lighter sled is that push athletes who have more physical bulk can then be used to help increase a team's push-start time without the overall sled weight being compromised.

With a promise to the U.S. bobsled athletes sketched out in his head, Geoff Bodine knew just who to call next. As if by psychic connection, Bob Cuneo, President of Chassis Dynamics in Oxford, Connecticut, knew why Geoff was calling even before the pitch had hit him. Cuneo and partner Bob "Vee" Vaillancourt had also been watching the Olympic bobsled coverage, and they had each come to a similar conclusion. So with a simple "Let's do it!" attitude, Bodine joined forces with his old friends at Chassis Dynamics to accomplish what many said was impossible.

The Chassis Dynamics team had more than 20 years' experience engineering world-renowned race cars, including Bodine's earlier NASCAR modified cars. More than 50 percent of all NASCAR Winston Modified Racing wins from 1984 to the present have been by Chassis Dynamics cars. From 1980 to 1984, nearly 50

Hans Kummer

Athletes Jim Herberich (left) and
Brian Shimer (right) with bobsled
crew chief Frank Briglia (center)
at Geoff Bodine's race shop, 1997

percent of all wins for the
NASCAR Modified Tour were
also Chassis Dynamics cars.
The team has designed,
produced, and developed
Oval Track, Road Race, Rally,
Drag Race, Snowmobile,
Motorcycle, and Midget
Racers which have won
hundreds of feature races,
broken dozens of track
records, and won scores of
track or divisional titles.

Both Cuneo and Vaillancourt were NASCAR modified drivers
and had competed regularly against their friend Bodine in the
early days of their careers. Sadly, "Vee" died in January 1996 of a
sudden illness. His innovative artistry as a master fabricator
combined with a mischievously quiet demeanor inspired many.
Vaillancourt's attention to detail, high moral standards, and
enduring friendship showed in the huge outpouring of sympathy
from the racing and bobsled communities upon his death.

Initially, Geoff Bodine spent $130,000 of his own money on a
prototype Bo-Dyn sled, and the Bobsled Project spent, in all,
more than $500,000 to develop and build six sleds. With state-
of-the-art computer assistance from IBM and aid from such
corporate sponsors as Dow/Corning, DuPont, the Family
Channel, Indianapolis Motor Speedway, and PPG Industries,
Chassis Dynamics was able to work its magic along with several
local Connecticut subcontractors and suppliers. With the help
of a grassroots volunteer fund-raising effort and donations from
individuals from across the country, the dream became a reality.
Within 18 months, from conception to product testing, the U.S.
team showed that it was back and ready to challenge the world
in bobsledding competition. (For more on the Bo-Dyn sled, see
Chapter 3, "The Sled.")

A New Era Dawns
The 1996–97 Season

During the 1996–97 season, the U.S. Bobsled Team broke track records and won a total of 13 medals in eight races. The team even made the bobsled history books. In the entire history of bobsled, no country has ever started a race in the third seed and finished in the top ten. This season the U.S. team did it *twice*, and in the second race took the gold medal.

The remarkable turnaround for the team was due, in part, to the redesigned Bo-Dyn bobsled and a change in how the athletes were grouped. The fastest athletes were matched with the fastest sleds. The USBSF adopted a fresh approach to the team sport concept and focused attention on the areas that coaches, athletes, and sponsors thought needed work.

The hard work paid off. Improvements included new coaches; new athletes (with an average age of 27); continually improved equipment; new sleds; a funded on-site crew chief for the first time; off-season fitness training; a residency program for top-performing athletes; and much-needed team funding.

Frank A. Posluszny

1998 U.S. two-man sleds at Chassis Dynamics—Oxford, Connecticut

There were certainly individual feats to highlight during the 1996–97 season, but most remarkable were the team's achievements as a whole. In the international rankings, the U.S. team took first place in two-man competition and third place in four-man competition.

The World Championships are a true test of ability, and the U.S. team faired well at the events in St. Moritz, Switzerland. For the first time since 1961, the United States won medals in both two-man and the four-man competition. Driver Brian Shimer and brakeman Rob Olesen finished third in the two-man competition. Shimer with side pushers Chip Minton and Randy Jones and brakeman Rob Olesen claimed the bronze medal and took home the Start Trophy (for fastest start time) in the four-man competition.

The team's confidence soared as it attacked the track in Nagano, Japan, during the last race of the World Cup season. Shimer took a gold and silver medal in four-man competition on the

©SKS/Seelmann

1996–97 U.S. Men's Bobsled Team

track, which made its Olympic debut in 1998. Jim Herberich took home silver in the two-man race and placed fifth in four-man competition.

The 1997–98 season

The 1997–98 World Cup and Olympic circuit for the U.S. men's team was fraught with high expectations, early promise, a turbulent midseason, and heartbreaking misfortune. In a series of unparalleled events, the men proved the old adage "Racin's Racin'"—meaning anything can happen, so expect the unexpected.

The season illustrated the principle that technically superior equipment, such as a Bo-Dyn bobsled, can only be an aid to the team. The ultimate path to victory lies in mental and physical preparation by each athlete individually and by the team as a whole. It is not easy for team members to keep a positive attitude under the pressure of international competition and the glare of media scrutiny.

The team elected not to attend the annual Monaco Push Championships, choosing instead to stay in Lake Placid to concentrate on team dynamics and training. The World Cup circuit started with a bang in Calgary, Alberta, Canada, as the two-man team of Brian Shimer and Randy Jones won the silver medal. Shimer pulled a hamstring during the push-start of the final heat, but used his driving skills to make up for the slow push time.

The season's second race, in Winterberg, Germany, saw the four-man team of Brian Shimer, Chip Minton, Randy Jones, and Garrett Hines take the gold. Shimer, still in pain from the previous week's hamstring pull, again made up record time with clean driving. The two-man teams of Shimer/Minton and Jim Herberich/Rob Olesen finished seventh and eighth, respectively.

The U.S. men then were off to Cortina d'Ampezzo, Italy, for the third race. The two-man team of Shimer/Hines tied with

Germany's Christoph Langen/Olaf Hampel for fourth place. The two-man USA III sled of Tuffy Latour and Jason Dorsey finished tenth. Brian Shimer's four-man team placed eighth. At the fourth World Cup competition in La Plagne, France, the two-man team of Herberich/Olesen rebounded from 12th place in the first heat to finish sixth. The Shimer/Jones team finished in tenth place. Shimer's four-man team took seventh.

Nancy Pierpoint

Team Shimer and the Spirit of New Jersey at the
1998 Olympic Trials

After Cortina, the U.S. men headed home for the holidays as well as to prepare for the U.S. Olympic Trials in Park City, Utah. The trial runs featured some competitive racing, as Tuffy Latour was ultimately replaced by Todd Hays to drive USA III for the remainder of the World Cup season and serve on the alternate team at the Olympics.

It was around this time that the world began to learn the reason behind the team's recent morale problems and lackluster results after a promising start. Athlete Brian Shimer, top contender for the nation's first Olympic bobsled medal in 42 years, was being investigated for the possible use of illegal steroid drugs. He was being reviewed for abnormally high levels of testosterone (a male hormone produced naturally in the body) and abnormally low readings of its counterpart, epitestosterone. Word of the private FIBT review leaked to the international competition.

For six weeks after the Calgary drug test, Shimer and the team were uncertain of the outcome. He was cleared by the FIBT medical commission shortly before the Olympics began, but the mental distractions took their toll on the team. "It worried me, it bothered me. I wasn't too focused after it came out. I hope people know I wouldn't be that stupid after 12 years of competing to all of a sudden try to get around the system," Shimer said.

Following the Park City trials, the team headed back to Europe for the fifth race in Igls, Austria. The two-man team of Shimer/Hines placed sixth, and Shimer's four-man team finished eighth. The final World Cup race in St. Moritz, Switzerland, saw the two-man team of Jim Herberich and John Kasper involved in a crash at the end of the track, but the duo ultimately took the bronze medal.

The 1997–98 international rankings put the U.S. team in fifth place in two-man competition and seventh place for four-man competition. In driver ranking, Brian Shimer placed sixth, Jim Herberich finished seventh, and Todd Hays placed 34th.

Shortly before the Nagano Olympic Games began, U.S. bobsledder Mike Dionne was put on temporary suspension for testing positive for the stimulant ephedrine. The banned substance is found in several over-the-counter cold medications. He had inadvertently taken a food supplement and cold medicine, both of which contained the stimulant, shortly before he was asked for a drug test. Most first-time offenders are given a simple warning, but in this case the penalty was more severe. Dionne, a side pusher for USA III, appealed his case to various review panels while the

Olympic Games proceeded. He was removed from the athlete village and could not train with his teammates. He did, however, retain his athlete status as a member of the American team.

Nagano Olympic Games, 1998

At Nagano, the U.S. team was consistently fast and competitive in the Olympic training runs. In the two-man competition, Jim Herberich and Robert Olesen improved every heat and finished the four-heat race in 3:38.53. The duo took seventh place. Brian Shimer and Garrett Hines combined to place tenth. Even before the Olympics, Shimer thought his medal chances were better in the four-man because his team's starts were better.

The four-man competition took place the following weekend. In a finish reminiscent of Brent Rushlaw's heartbreak at Calgary in 1988, Brian Shimer and his crew of Nathan Minton, Randy Jones, and Garrett Hines missed a bronze medal by two one-hundredths of a second. They missed a silver medal by seven one-hundredths of a second.

After the first heat on Friday, Shimer and crew had the second fastest start of the day and were in fourth place. The second heat, which was scheduled for Friday, was canceled due to heavy rain and sleet. After heat two, held the next day, Shimer drove his crew to a tie for third place with Great Britain's sled of Sean Olsson, Dean Ward, Courtney Rumbolt, and Paul Attwood. When Great Britain and Switzerland faltered in the third and final heat, Shimer saw his chance. The crew had the best push time of the day at 4.90 seconds. Three-quarters of the way down the track, he was leading by nearly two-tenths of a second. After tapping a wall, the sled began to lose speed and couldn't regain it. The final split time showed him ahead, but within the final 15 seconds of the heat, the sled had lost just enough momentum to cross the finish line out of medal contention. The USA II team of Jim Herberich, Darrin Steele, John Kasper, and Rob Olesen finished in 12th position.

Nancy Pierpoint

Jim Herberich and the Spirit of Connecticut in Park City, Utah

Looking to the Future

Fierce international competition keeps the U.S. Bobsled Team fighting for more speed and strength. American bobsledders continue to face formidable challenges from powerful teams from Canada, Germany, Italy, and Switzerland.

The 2000–01 season buoyed America's hopes for the upcoming Olympic Games. With Brian Shimer hampered by a knee injury during the National Team trials, driver Todd Hays and his crew rose to the occasion to win the trials and go into international competition as USA I. Hays and his crew of Pavle Jovanovic, Randy Jones, and Garrett Hines collected top-ten finishes in four-man races throughout the world; their best finishes were fourths at Igls and Calgary. In the World Cup at Lake Placid, Hays led brakeman Pavle Jovanovic to their first medal ever as a two-man team. The duo won a bronze on the new Mt. Van

Jason Leon

Team Hays celebrates after winning their first World Cup event in March 2001, ending a four-year gold medal drought by the U.S. Men's Team.

Hoevenberg track. The following day, Hays was determined to prove the Lake Placid track worthy of hosting the event. (There was some speculation concerning the safety of the new facility.) Hays and crew rallied from a fifth-place ranking after the first heat to win the World Cup finale. This was Hays's first career victory on the World Cup circuit. USA II driver Mike Dionne collected two sixth-place finishes at Lake Placid.

Women's Bobsledding—An Uphill Climb

The story of women's bobsledding is one that can appeal to everyone. After years of competing with men on the early co-ed bobsled teams, women were banned from the sport. When the ban was temporarily lifted, Katharine Dewey (granddaughter of Melvil Dewey, inventor of the Dewey Decimal System for classifying library books) won a national championship as the driver for a co-ed team. Unfortunately, the decision to allow women to compete was reversed shortly after her victory.

A new day for female sliders dawned in October 1999, when the International Olympic Committee announced that women's bobsledding would be added to the 2002 Winter Olympic Games as a full medal sport.

The Champ Was a Lady

The history of women's participation in the organized sport of bobsledding dates back to 1897, when the St. Moritz Bobsleigh Club was founded. This club was one of the world's first organized bob associations, and it served as an impetus for cultivating the sport. The club's British organizers had more than bobsledding in mind: they also wanted to foster the emancipation of women. To that end, they made sure the club rules specified that two of the five-member board of directors had to be women. The club also required at least two women on each four-person race team and a minimum of one on a three-person bob team. This ruling was internationally accepted until 1924, when it was decided that women were no longer capable of participating because of the danger associated with increased track speeds. Prior to this decision, there were also occasional women-only and men-only races.

The Amateur Athletic Union (AAU) was created in 1888 to correct widespread problems in amateur athletics in the United States. In 1940 the AAU reopened the sport of bobsledding to

Circa 1940 archive photo
Katharine Dewey (second from left) and other female bobsledders

women. Days after this decision was made, Katharine Dewey won the U.S. National Four-Man Bobsled Championship. In doing so, Dewey became the only woman in the history of bobsledding, or any other sport, to win a national title in open competition against men. Unfortunately, her victory was short-lived. The AAU reversed its decision and said women could only compete against women, effectively banning them from sanctioned competition.

Creating the Sport of Tomorrow, Today

In 1994 the USBSF decided it was time to get women back on the track. It placed newspaper ads all over the country to spread the word and attract potential athletes. Hundreds of applications later, 16 women were invited to try out.

Eight talented athletes were chosen for the first team. They came from diverse sports backgrounds (including soccer, volleyball, taekwondo, basketball, and track) and were dedicated to learning bobsledding techniques. Two athletes even qualified for the National Team while pregnant. This first group set the standard for teams to follow.

From the beginning, the American public has recognized and sympathized with the team's struggles, sacrifices, and pursuit of excellence. Like the Jamaican Bobsled Team in *Cool Runnings*, these women have struggled against the odds and are continually overcoming obstacles. They started from scratch, organized a team from nothing, and now compete at a high level on an international racing circuit.

Unlike sports such as women's gymnastics, where competitors tend to be young, female bobsledders range in age from teenagers to women in their forties. The 2000–01 U.S. Women's Bobsled Team had members between 22 and 40 years old, with diverse backgrounds and professions.

The 1996–97 season

The U.S. women's team made significant progress in growth and recognition during the 1996–97 season. A record number of athletes tried out for the team. Their training schedule was longer than in the past, and they completed an outstanding World Cup season. The number-one U.S. women's sled placed fifth in the world overall. Even more impressive was the increase in the skill of the women drivers around the world. The overall difference between the second- and fifth-place sleds was less than half a second.

Of primary importance was the signing of a major sponsor for the team—American Skandia Insurance. In addition to continuing financial support, American Skandia provided corporate and media exposure for the team and funded the purchase of youth sleds for the Park City track. This latter action was favorably received by the USOC, as it will help promote the USOC's Community Olympic Development Center in the Salt Lake City area.

The 1997–98 season

The 1997–98 women's program was vastly improved over previous years. Two training camps were held, which allowed the athletes to learn more of the push technique. All of the qualified athletes improved their six-item test scores from previous years. In November the team moved to Park City, Utah, to train. Through additional funding from American Skandia, the women were able to purchase a 1997 Dresden two-person sled. They hired a coach for the entire season and were provided with housing, uniforms, food allowance, and upgraded equipment while in Park City.

On the World Cup circuit, the team participated at four different race venues and returned home with one gold medal (won on the Park City track) and three silver medals. The United States

Courtesy of USBSF

1997–98 U.S. Women's Bobsled Team
Left to right: Krista Ford, Sue Blazejewski, Jean Racine, Jill Bakken,
Meg Henderson, Elena Primerano

ranked third overall in the Women's World Cup standings. Jean Racine placed fourth in the driver standings, while Jill Bakken placed seventh. It should be noted that neither driver competed in the full circuit of racing.

The season got under way with two push competitions in Europe. The team of Jill Bakken and Elena Primerano won the gold in Gotha, Germany. In the Monaco Push Championships, the team of Sue Blazejewski and Krista Ford took the silver medal.

The first two competitions the team participated in were held at Calgary, Alberta, and Park City, Utah. The American women played host to their international competitors at the Park City race. Following Park City, Bakken and Primerano were invited to a Japan Women's Friendly Cup race at Mount Fuji Bobsleigh Land. While the race was not a true World Cup event, the trip provided a tremendous opportunity for the international women's teams to get to know one another better.

Due to a lack of funding, only one team was able to compete in the race in Igls, Austria. Poor performance and a sixth-place finish emphasized that the team as a whole needed more track time on the world's various bobruns. A serious crash in training by a British team forced the cancellation of the next race in La Plagne, France. A generous monetary contribution by Racine's father enabled the team of Racine and Ford to join the team of Bakken and Primerano at La Plagne. The two teams went back to Igls to get in some additional track time before heading off to the season's final race in Winterberg, Germany.

Courtesy of USBSF

Pushing the extremes: U.S. women
bobsledders take to the ice.

The 2000–01 Season

The 2000–01 team collected medals from all over the world and enjoyed the women's most successful season to date. Driver Jean Racine won the 1999–2000 and 2000–01 season titles, after finishing the 1998–99 season in second place behind Switzerland's Francoise Burdet. Racine combined with Jen Davidson to win six

Julie Urbansky- USBSF

Members of the U.S. Women's Bobsled Team celebrate their medal sweep at the 2001 Park City World Cup. *Left to right:* Vonetta Flowers, Bonny Warner, Jean Racine, Jen Davidson, Jill Bakken, Kristi McGihon

of the seven World Cup races during 2000–01. Driver Bonny Warner finished the season third in World Cup points. Driver Jill Bakken, although hampered by injuries, ranked ninth in World Cup standings.

In February 2001, the U.S. Women's Bobsled Team accomplished an amazing feat, one that brought tears to all those who have pushed to get recognition for women's bobsledding. The team placed first, second, and third at the 2001 Park City World Cup Finale. The test event for the 2002 Winter Olympic Games saw Jean Racine and Jen Davidson win the gold medal and clinch the season title.

3

The Sled

Today's modern bobsled is an aerodynamic vehicle made of fiberglass and steel, mounted on four highly polished steel runners. The two front runners have approximately three inches of lateral movement and are steered by two ropes attached to D-shaped rings held by the driver. The brake handles are located on either side of the brakeman in the four-man sled and in front of the brakeman in the two-man sled. When pulled, the lever lowers a saw-toothed brake bar that digs into the ice.

A bobsled's speed is affected by three main factors: the push-start, weight, and air/ice friction. All things being equal, the heaviest sled and crew combination will run the fastest. To equalize competition, the FIBT in 1985 introduced new sled requirements. Under the new rules, four-man sleds and crews cannot exceed a total of 1,388 pounds, and sleds cannot be more than 12.47 feet long. Two-man sleds and occupants may have a total weight up to 860 pounds, and sleds may have a maximum length of 8.85 feet. Lighter crews can add weight bars to their sleds before a race to achieve the maximum weight; however, a heavier sled has proven to be more difficult to push-start.

It is illegal to heat the runners to make the sled go faster. The temperature of each team's sled runners is taken electronically

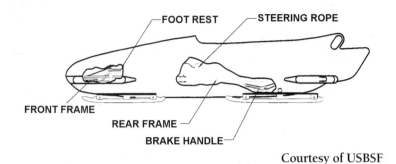

Courtesy of USBSF

immediately prior to each race. At the finish line, the sled and crew are weighed to ensure that they are below the maximum weight.

The Genesis

Archaeological evidence indicates that ancient peoples used sleds as transportation as early as 15,000 years ago, even before the invention of the wheel. The ancient sled consisted of animal skin stretched between two pieces of wood. The next major step was taken during the reign of the Roman Empire. One-man hand-pulled sleds were invented to carry supplies and mail, a custom that was also followed by North American Indian tribes. The Eskimos conceived the practical notion of hitching a hand sled to their dogs.

As early as the 1830s, single and double "bobbed" hand sleds were used by American and Canadian lumberjacks to transport timber and gear through the dense forest. The use of an individual hand sled for recreational sliding (tobogganing) became popular in the 1870s with Canadian timbermen and at Russian winter carnivals.

What started as friends racing against each other quickly began to take shape as an official sport. In 1877 a group of American and British tourists on vacation near Davos, Switzerland, modified a hand sled and raced down the Swiss slopes. The

British held the first Davos International Race in 1883. The race consisted of 21 international competitors who slid down a two-mile slope. A year later, the Grand National toboggan race was held in St. Moritz, attracting 20 competitors.

Bobsled's Cradle: The United States

While the Swiss were enjoying tobogganing in the late 1870s and the 1880s, the Americans were tinkering with the lumberjacks' bobsled design. The timbermen in the Albany area began to modify their transport sled, which consisted of a wooden plank joining two hand sleds, with the front sled being able to pivot from side to side. They mounted a "steering" wheel to the front wooden runners and connected a "brake" or "tiller" wheel to the rear runners.

Just as tobogganing quickly grew from racing against friends to become an organized sport, so too did bobsledding. By 1882, numerous bob clubs had formed to challenge each other. The sport was now open to all interested individuals (men, women, and children) who could build a sled and organize a team. The Albany Bobbing (Coasting) Association was soon formed to organize the many clubs taking shape in the area.

By 1886 the Association was gaining national media attention by holding the annual Bobbers' Carnival. The winter carnival activities included a bobbers' parade (the first of its kind in the United States) with more than 80 bobsleds on display, as well as multiple races. Such festivals drew people from many different geographic areas, and a separate racing division was created specifically for visiting bob clubs.

The year 1886 also saw dramatic changes in sled design. Gone were the simple wooden planks. They were replaced by fresh paint and varnish, metal plating, cushions, lantern headlights, steel brakes, and individual steering modifications. Many of the bobs were decorated with bright streamers and ribbons attached to long ropes dragging behind the sled. Some were also adorned with attractive canopies, lanterns, flowers, and evergreens, and with the club's name, motto, or emblem.

Albany bobbing quickly surpassed all other area amusements in the number of participants and spectators. The question of which bob would be considered champion was a favorite topic of yearly debate. The 40-foot-long Tachistos (meaning "swiftest") was jokingly named the "Snail" after it repeatedly reached record speeds of up to 60 mph. The Brooklyn Bridge Club took pride in its 800-pound, 30-man sled. The $700 Frazier bob from Syracuse continually attracted much attention, and the 28-foot sled of the Beaver Yak Club was an annual favorite.

The sleds raced on the snow-packed downhill streets of Albany. Newspaper accounts in the *Albany Evening Union* refer to the Frazier bob that "... reached Eagle Street in nineteen seconds, Philip Street in twenty-four seconds and crossed the Pearl Street [finish] line in forty-four seconds." However, it was only a matter of time before high speeds, heavy equipment, multiple riders, and pedestrian-lined streets made for a disastrous mix.

The end came on February 2, 1889, when a sled careened out of control and plunged into a crowd of spectators on South Pearl Street. One young man was killed, and several other people were injured. As a result, the mayor of Albany stopped that year's carnival and permanently barred the city from hosting the event. This brought a halt to the early period of U.S. bobsled preeminence.

The Evolution

While bobsledding faced an uncertain future in the United States, the Europeans began wholeheartedly to embrace the pastime. The posh villas and spas of Switzerland sought to emulate the Albany experience and, soon after, an international sport began to take shape. In 1889 two Swiss men—Major Bulpett and Christian Mathis—created the first multiseat steel bobsled with rope steering instead of a wheel. It did not have brakes and was stopped with the aid of a garden rake.

Albany Evening News, NY, 1886

"…Long before the revived Olympics were thought of, Albany's boys
were building and using bobsleds…"

The Swiss sleds did not have the length or weight of the first
American sleds that carried as many as 30 people. The newer
sleds did away with the rear wheel and were ridden by three
to six people.

Early competitions also allowed team members to straddle their
sleds, sitting upright or lying flat on top of each other, just as an
individual toboggan rider would. The lying-down method
became the style of choice and raised heated discussions for
many years, particularly from "wholesome" ladies. The debate
between prone sledders and sitting sledders was particularly
volatile during the 1910–11 St. Moritz racing season. The face-
down/headfirst style reached its peak in the 1920s and was
abolished from the sport by the FIBT in 1930–31.

As the sport expanded throughout Europe, so too did the need
for more and better equipment. Several bobsled manufacturers
established themselves in Switzerland.

Christian Mathis continued to build steel sleds in St. Moritz into the 1920s, when August Hartkopf of Davos became the largest exporter of steel sleds. The Bachman Brothers in Travers also gained wide acceptance with their wooden sleds and a steering wheel instead of conventional ropes. Although car-like steering was embraced for quite a while, it was ultimately abandoned. The linear motion of the ropes and handles proved to be the most direct steering method, since it was unaffected by rapid roll rates through sequential turns. It also allowed the driver to pull hard with both hands, which was about all he had available to keep him in the sled.

As in most industries, the technological evolution of the bobsled involved a process of trial and error. Advances in the automobile industry at the turn of the century and then again in the 1930s and '40s prompted the return of the steering wheel, as well as numerous advances in aerodynamics, safety, and materials. Carl Feierabend of Engelberg, Switzerland, designed a series of streamlined sleds that dominated the sport from the 1930s through the 1950s.

The modern bobsled began to take shape in the mid-1950s, as Siorpaes created Italian bobsleds with a two-part frame (chassis). The two parts allowed the front portion of the sled to be flexible and move independently of the rear. This created more stability, allowing all four runners to be in contact with the ice at the same time. The Italian sleds held a monopoly on sled construction during the 1960s and '70s. Several countries, including England and France, tried to create their own new versions, but all failed to match the Italians' superiority. The United States, in partnership with General Motors, also mounted a challenge, but to no avail.

The period from the late 1970s to the mid-1980s saw the resurgence of individual team research and development, particularly in relation to aerodynamics and the use of resin materials. The East Germans and Swiss dominated with enclosed sled sides and modifications to individual parts, including runners and push handles. East Germany and the Soviet Union also began using wind tunnel testing on new body designs. Their work showed at the 1984 Winter Olympics in Sarajevo. The Soviets raced fast cigar-shaped sleds that were hard to steer; the East German sleds had individually suspended runners. Because of many irregularities at the Olympics that year, the FIBT was forced to adopt sled standardization measurements and procedures for all international teams. Sleds of Italian and German manufacture continue to be the top choice of European bobsled teams.

In 1983 the USOC formed the Sports Equipment and Technology Committee, which provides research funding and acts as a liaison between sports, industry, and government. The 1988 Winter Olympics in Calgary saw the debut of composite material sleds with integrated chassis and body that could adapt to both hard and soft ice tracks. Premiering in Calgary was a U.S. sled designed by Airflow Sciences Corp. of Livonia, Michigan. The $1.8-million project was funded partly by the USOC and featured a few radical design changes. These included replacing the steel chassis with a high-strength, drag-reducing body made of fiberglass honeycomb sandwiched between carbon fiber; adding a metal articulation ring that allowed the two halves of the sled to move completely independent of each other; and suspending the team members in webbing one-half inch above the sled floor and padding them in with foam to reduce movement and increase stability. While noble in effort and novel in concept, the sled was deemed undrivable because the independent articulation meant the sled would move in two different directions in a turn, almost always causing a crash.

The Bo-Dyn Revolution

Over the years, several American patrons and corporations have unsuccessfully tried to develop new sled technology. For the most part, each group's research did not quite grasp the subtle yet complex mechanics and rhythm of bobsledding. This situation changed in 1992, when Geoff Bodine contracted with Chassis Dynamics to develop a new bobsled. In just a year and a half of intensive effort, Chassis Dynamics built six Bo-Dyn sleds and took the world by storm.

The first real research and development period for the sleds was the 1994 Winter Olympics in Lillehammer. Despite media claims to the contrary, the team was not vying for medal contention, but rather wanted to test the Bo-Dyn sled's capabilities under real-time competition constraints.

The main U.S. four-man sled was disqualified for having runners that were too warm just prior to race time. Despite the team's contrary temperature indications, the official judgment stood, and the team became the first in history to be disqualified for "hot" runners.

During the 1994–95 World Cup season, the Chassis Dynamics team evaluated previous performance and modified the sleds on a shoestring budget. The improved sleds gave the U.S. team two World Cup medals.

Overview of the Bo-Dyn sled

The following is an overview of a Bo-Dyn bobsled's main features.

Body construction: A Kevlar® composite weave (Kevlar is a registered product of DuPont). Its aerodynamic shape was wind-tunnel tested and designed by Boeing engineers and U.S. bobsledder Brian Richardson. It was further developed and built by Chassis Dynamics.

Chassis construction: Steel alloy tubing, designed and built by Chassis Dynamics.

Suspension: A four-layered suspension. The front of the sled can rotate independently from the rear of the sled (this is called articulation). The front axle pivots longitudinally. The shoes, which hold the runners, can twist over bumps while allowing small vertical movement. Designed and built by Chassis Dynamics.

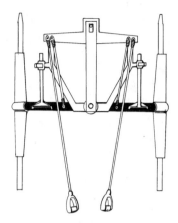

Steering: Steering of the sled occurs through two D-shaped handles connected to a steering system through a bungee cord, cable, and linkage network. The bungee cord provides a dampening layer between high-speed movements of the sled and the driver's hands.

Illustrated by Frank Posluszny

Runner Design and Preparation

A sled builder can select from a million different combinations of alloy composition, forging techniques, and shape design to produce a batch of steel runners. Yet within any particular group, one set of runners might be fast in cold, dry conditions and another set may be snail slow in anything but warm, wet conditions. In the past, U.S. athletes had to buy runners from European manufacturers.

Today, Crucible Specialty Metals of Syracuse, New York, is using its state-of-the-art particle metal forging techniques to make runners that have predictable and reproducible capabilities. This application of metallurgical expertise to the sport, it is hoped, will give the U.S. team another advantage over its European competitors. Additionally, Bob Cuneo of Chassis Dynamics recruited Advance Manufacturing (Westfield, Mass.), Aerospace

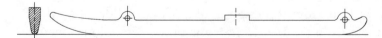

RUNNER PROFILE
ROUND BOTTOM   BOBSLED RUNNER SIDE VIEW

Illustrated by Frank Posluszny

Alloys (Manchester, Conn.), Automation Development (Burlington, Conn.), and United Precision (Salt Lake City, Utah) to assist in runner production.

Each athlete on a four-man team is responsible for preparing the four runners for race day. This is a process that can take well over three hours. An athlete begins sanding with the coarsest sandpaper and works his way to the finest grit. The steel runner stores the heat of all the continuous rubbing. The challenge, then, is to cool the runner enough to comply with the temperature bounds set by the FIBT.

Team Provolone's Revenge

Through continued evaluation and modification, the U.S. Bobsled Team has been gaining momentum with its Bo-Dyn bobsled. During the 2000–01 season, the U.S. men finally earned the gold medal that they were anxiously awaiting. Driver Todd Hays and his crew of Pavle Jovanovic, Randy Jones, and Garrett Hines achieved the feat at the 2001 World Cup in Lake Placid, New York. The new track at Mt. Van Hoevenberg proved difficult for many of the competitors, but Hays and crew rose to the challenge, taking the gold in the four-man competition. The women's team drove the Bo-Dyn to greater heights during the 2000–01 season, with Jean Racine and Jen Davidson combining to win six of the seven World Cup events in a Bo-Dyn sled.

The brains behind America's brawny sled technology can be found among a unique group of friends from Connecticut. Dubbed by the American athletes as "Team Provolone," for their mainly Italian heritage, this group revolutionized bobsled design by approaching their task from a new angle. As racing enthusiasts, they each applied their own distinctive brand of expertise to the project, in order to design, build, paint, and detail all the Bo-Dyn sleds in the U.S. fleet. Some of the "Provolone" members even function as crew chief and pit crew for the U.S. Bobsled Team while on tour.

The 1994 debut of the Bo-Dyn sled was laughed at by many in the international community. The fact that the four-man Olympic sled was disqualified from competition for having runners that were too warm added further insult to injury for those who had given and dedicated so much of their lives to the project.

The tide turned during the 1996–97 World Cup season, and Team Provolone made further improvements in the Bo-Dyn design after the USBSF decided to buy a German Dresden sled for study. The Chassis Dynamics team then took it apart, analyzed it, and figured out what made it fast. The end result became the second-generation Bo-Dyn sled.

Nancy Pierpoint

Team Provolone's 1998 family photo

The Bo-Dyn II actually combines the best of two technologies— a hybrid of the original Bo-Dyn and the German Dresden. Bob Cuneo at Chassis Dynamics mounted the fine-tuned chassis and suspension of the Bo-Dyn in a modified Dresden shape. The second-generation sleds also include a new push bar design that enables the teams to load more efficiently and reduce push-start times.

The rear push bars have been raised, and the driver's push bar is extended for better leverage. A lower rear seat pan positions the crew more aerodynamically in the sled. Still, the key to victory may lie in the Bo-Dyn's weight, which is about 150 pounds lighter than a traditional sled. The reduced load allows for a brawnier crew who can generate more power at the start. All the evidence—including test data, medals won, and track records broken—seems to indicate that the new Bo-Dyn II is the world's best all-around competitive sled.

4

Clothing and Safety

Guidelines and rules governing clothing and safety were not established until the 1920s. Men typically wore thick wool caps pulled down to expose only their eyes and noses to the cold. Sweaters, elbow-length gloves, leggings made of sailcloth or leather, and high hiking boots were also common attire.

Early on, women wore long skirts, long winter coats with hoods, high-top boots, and usually broad-brimmed hats tied with scarves. Eventually, female sledders wore the same clothing that they would wear to go skiing, such as toboggan suits or sweaters.

In addition to decorating their sleds, members of the early bob clubs also dressed to impress. Individual groups created team uniforms reflecting the name of their bobsled, such as The Mikados (Japanese), The Not Left (orphans), and My Aunt Bridget. Many clubs wore stylized toboggan racing suits or costumes reflecting the club's theme. Otherwise, emblems representing a club were worn on sweaters, and a brightly colored sash with the team name in big letters completed the look. The teams would display their sled and crew during a parade prior to racing and compete for silk pennants with designated dollar values.

The prizes included:

Best Decorated Bob: 1st prize/$30
2nd prize/$20

Best All-Around Bob: 1st prize/$20
2nd prize/$14
3rd prize/$10

Best Uniformed Club: 1st prize/$25
2nd prize/$15

Bobsledding Safety

In 1886 the *Albany Argus* newspaper printed a business notice from The Travelers Insurance Company stating that "Bob sledding and tobogganing and all accidents are paid under [our] policies."

Athlete safety concerns about using the early "open-air" sleds were addressed by adding simple protective devices to the sled itself, including runners with iron struts and seat cushions. Hand and belt loops that provided grip and body stabilization were lauded in the "advanced" Italian sleds of the 1950s.

Sledders started wearing protective helmets between 1920 and 1930. Helmets became FIBT regulation items in the early 1930s and were made of compressed cardboard, plywood, leather, and other assorted materials. The athletes also began to wear elbow and knee pads made of leather or felt.

It is important to note that the early addition of a front nose cowling to a sled was mainly a protective feature for the driver. The use of cowls was well observed before 1920, yet as the automobile industry streamlined, so too did bobsled design. The cowling was now considered an aerodynamic feature. Safety was put on hold, and decreasing wind resistance became the key.

The use of rigid synthetic resins in bobsled construction in the mid-1950s brought a residual improvement in athlete safety.

Each team began to build its own custom-tailored sled body, a practice still in effect today. In fact, the members of the 1957 four-man World Championship team constructed their sled in a kitchen. Unfortunately, they found that the sled was too big to go through the room's narrow doors. The use of resin materials helped provide the start of the modern bobsled era with sturdy sled bodies that enclosed the athletes during a bobrun.

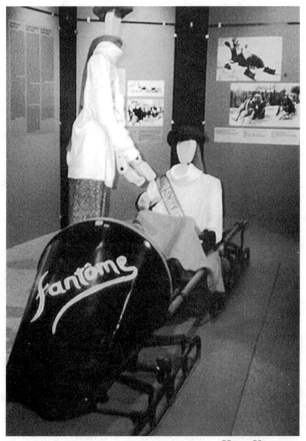

Hans Kummer

Swiss Sports Museum traveling exhibition featuring early 20th century bobsled attire and "modern" advances in bobsled design

The Modern Age

Today's bobsledders use a wide variety of high-tech safety equipment and accessories.

Helmets

Today's sledders wear full-head helmets made of the super strong and rigid material Kevlar® (bulletproof vests and Bo-Dyn bobsleds are also made of this DuPont material). Drivers' helmets usually have a clear plastic shield that can pivot down to cover their faces.

Average cost: Helmet—$300–800

Start Shoes

These are a special variation of the shoes worn for track and field. Made particularly for use in ice sports by Adidas, they have 500 tiny spikes on the ball of the foot. The spikes ensure a tight grip on the ice as the athletes run in unison at top speed to gain a fast push-start. Spike covers are also needed to protect the spikes prior to the race.

Average cost: Spikes—$125–250; Covers—$40–60

Speed Suits

These are one-piece suits, usually made of a nylon-Lycra® blend with a rubberized outer coating to protect the athlete. The suits are skintight, yet stretch to allow the slider to have complete freedom of movement. They also provide minimal warmth via body heat and are an aerodynamic element needed to make a push-start as fast as possible.

Average cost: $160–200

Abrasion Vest

This piece of protective gear typically is made of padded nylon. It protects the athlete in the event of an accident and, even more important, provides a stable and rigid support structure for the athlete's body when a sled enters a curve and pressures of four, five, and even six times the force of gravity are exerted. Some athletes also choose to wear elbow and shoulder padding over their racing suits.

Average cost: $135

Gloves

Most bobsledders wear lightweight racing gloves for further protection and warmth. Some drivers prefer to use bare hands for a better feel of the steering ropes.

Average cost: $25

5

Youth Programs and Recruitment

Youth Services

The USBSF's Youth Development Program, the Sports Development Department of the New York State Olympic Regional Development Authority in Lake Placid, and the Utah Olympic Park in Park City are working together to build a bridge to the future.

The United States is one of a very few nations that actively seek to involve boys and girls in bobsledding. Typically, countries participating in international bobsledding competition rely on the recruitment of athletes in their late teens and twenties who have established abilities in other sports. While the United States also follows this practice, the USBSF and the USOC wish to continue developing a diverse group of new bobsled competitors. By educating and developing young athletes, the organizations believe they will make U.S. bobsledders the best in the world. Several unique programs tailored to young athletes have been introduced.

The Bobsledding Push Clinic

Children can participate in this "Olympic Sports Fantasy Camp" during the spring, summer, and fall months. Trained coaches and athletes guide children through the basics of bobsledding. Alternative sport activities such as mountain biking and inline skating are also available.

The Blind Odyssey Program

This event is designed to expose blind children to the experience of bobsledding. One-on-one interaction with coaches and Pee Wee athletes as both "instructor" and teammate help ensure fun, safety, friendship, and hands-on cooperative learning. Highlighting the event, the blind athletes slide down the bottom portion of the bobrun in a junior bobsled with a Pee Wee athlete at the helm.

The Pee Wee Junior Bobsled Program

This fast-growing event lets hundreds of kids from ages 8 to 17 experience the thrill of bobsledding one evening each week during the winter season. Pee Wees generally slide the last 300 yards of the bobrun in specially designed two-person junior bobsleds. The Pee Wee season concludes with kids competing for lightweight and heavyweight championship titles.

Bobstarting

This is a program that can be offered to children across the country. It involves teaching young people the fundamentals of bobsledding and the push-start. Each event is organized as either an interactive "show and tell" session or as a competition, in which children "push" a junior bobsled from point A to point B while being timed.

John Morgan

Jim and John Morgan with a friend at the
1957 Pee Wee Championships in Lake Placid

The junior sled can be pushed on ice, perhaps at a local rink.
Alternatively, the sled can be modified to run on rubber wheels
at any gym, civic hall, or other appropriate venue. To further
develop this activity, the USBSF Youth Program intends to provide
plans and specifications for the construction of a "bobstarting"

sled for elementary and junior high school athletic directors. Once a school or youth program has built a sled, it will be encouraged to organize a competition.

Although in existence for several years, the USBSF Youth Development Program is still in its infancy. There are many other possibilities to develop, and much room for growth in current activities. If you wish to learn more, get involved, or contribute, contact the USBSF's Youth Development Committee.

Gregory W. Borzilleri

Pee Wee bobsledders racing at Lake Placid

U.S. Bobsled Team Tryouts

Because the sport of bobsledding had received minimal media coverage in past years, it had acquired a "mystique" by the early 1990s. In 1993 the USBSF decided to take bobsledding to U.S. cities to capitalize on the public's growing fascination with the sport and to educate people about the athletes and equipment. The goal was to bring the sport within people's reach and allow them to test their interests and ability. The plan worked. The program was so popular that separate age categories were established, allowing entrants to compare their strength and skill levels with those of others in the same age bracket.

In these events, potential athletes individually push a sled from a standing start. Five meters down the track from the start blocks, they trip the first timing eye. The athletes are then measured as to how fast they push the sled from the first timing eye to the second timing eye/finish line, which is a distance of 20 meters. They then enter a braking area of 25 meters, during which the sled is slowed to a stop.

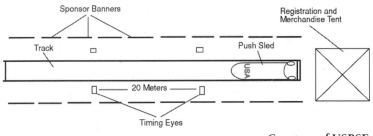

Courtesy of USBSF

The push sled used by the public is an actual competition two-man bobsled that has been modified to run on wheels rather than steel runners and weighs slightly more than 340 pounds. The push track is composed of 20 8' x 1' interlocking plywood sections with steel rails. A rubber/urethane running surface is placed over the plywood to form a firm, stable, and safe area for people of all abilities.

Most participants who score above the set qualifying time come to the event with no idea whether they have what it takes to be a bobsledder. While watching participants try to beat the clock, audience members become hooked and are unable to resist the challenge of testing their own abilities. In Seaside Heights, New Jersey, Jason Dorsey was on the beach with friends who dared him to push the sled. Sensing a challenge, Jason pushed (in sandals, no less); not only was he good enough to win his age category for the event, but he also received an invitation to the Olympic Training Center in Lake Placid. There he passed the required six-item speed and strength test for team qualification. Jason competed on the U.S. Men's National Team for many seasons.

Push sled competition is available nationwide from spring to fall, and is open to participants of all ages. For a small donation, participants register, sign a waiver, and wait in line to push.

Hans Kummer

Cool Running: A potential team
member at the official team tryouts

The all-day event may have one or more qualified athletes present to offer assistance and answer questions. Each participant is given an autographed card that includes his or her finish time, signed by a bobsled team athlete. Awards for the top three fastest in each of the four men's and women's age categories (12 and under, 13–18, 19–39, over 40) are mailed to the winners.

Any participant beating the set standard time (men's and women's times differ) will be allowed to attend a U.S. Bobsled Team Training Camp at the Olympic Training Center in Lake Placid, where he or she will try to qualify for the U.S. squad. Room and board will be provided at the beginning of the camp pending qualification. Transportation is the responsibility of the participant.

Courtesy of USBSF

Pee Wee bobstarting in Lake Placid

Targeting Prime and Future Athletes

The USBSF is working to expand the USOC's Community Olympic Development Centers program by reaching out to two types of athletes.

Prime Target Athletes

These are men and women from 18 to 27 years old who are already skilled in other sports such as baseball, football, and track. Male athletes typically weigh 180–230 pounds, while female athletes generally weigh 120–170 pounds. They are powerful and explosive, with very good hand-eye coordination. They should also be able to run a 40-yard dash in approximately 4.7 seconds.

These athletes should start training immediately. Their training consists of sport education, dry-land start training, bobsled simulator driver training, team planning, and bobsled mechanics.

Future Target Athletes

These boys and girls, ages 8 to 17, have an interest in becoming bobsledders. They must be athletically aggressive, yet coachable, with a desire to become the best they can be. They should have a background in a sport that develops strong lower-body abilities and good hand-eye coordination, such as track and field, football, baseball, softball, soccer, basketball, or skiing.

The USBSF's six-item physical fitness test is still the best model for determining whether an athlete has the ability to become a successful bobsledder. However, a young athlete may become discouraged if he or she lacks the technique to perform one of the events. One alternative might be to reduce the six-item test to perhaps a three-item test, including a 30-meter sprint, vertical jump, and three hops. Such a test might be a better measure of a young athlete's abilities and could be scaled for different age groups. This model may be implemented as the community of future athletes continues to grow.

How to Make the Men's Team

Anyone who is interested in becoming a bobsled athlete should contact the USBSF to inquire about tryouts, training camps, driving schools, coaching, and physical training.

The Basics

To qualify for the team you must:

- Be at least 18 years of age and in good physical condition.
- Be an athlete member of the USBSF by paying the annual fee and completing the Athlete Membership Application, as well as the Physical Form and Proof of Insurance card.
- Sign and accept the Athlete's Contract, Code of Conduct, and Bobsled Team Criteria Form.
- Be available to compete for the entire bobsled season.

To Become a Push Athlete

Unlike any other Olympic sport, bobsledding allows a push athlete—that is, a side pusher or brakeman—who has exceptional strength and speed to make the U.S. National Team in the first or second year. Here is what you need to do:

- Train for the USBSF's six-item test, which evaluates speed and strength. Take the test with a USBSF official and score above the minimum of 750 points.
- Attend one of the three seven-day summer push sled training camps at the U.S. Olympic Training Center in Lake Placid. (The push sleds have wheels instead of runners and glide on rails.) At the camp, you will train for and complete the following:
    1. The six-item test *again*, plus a three-item strength test (squat, power clean, and bench press)
    2. Push sled training
    3. The annual U.S. National Push Sled Championships

You may be picked by one of the U.S. drivers to join a four-man bobsled team based on:

- Your best score on the six-item test
- Your performance at a summer push sled training camp
- Your performance at the annual U.S. National Push Sled Championships.

The Six Item Test

Events (in their preferred running order)
1. 30 Meter Sprints   4. Vertical Jump
2. 60 Meter Sprints   5. Five Hops
3. 100 Meter Sprints   6. Shot Put Throw
All events are best of three attempts. Athletes are not required to take all three attempts.

Equipment Requirements:
Tape measure (preferably 50 meters)
Electronic timing
16 lb. shot put (8 lb. for women)
Vertical jump measuring equipment (Vertec preferred)

1. 30 Meters Sprint:
Set up: A 1 1/2" - 2" lip is placed one meter back from the start line (a sprint block will work, or a piece of tape will work if a rigid lip is not available). The eyes are set up on the inside of lane one and the reflectors are set up on the outside of lane three. The start eye is placed over the start line. The finish eye is at 30 meters.
The Event: The athletes may not start behind the rear one meter line (they may have one or both balls of their feet on the lip). They may not touch either hand to the ground. The competitiors typically take three sprint attempts. All times should be recorded. Once again, only the fastest of the three attempts is scored.

2. 60 Meters Sprint:
Set up: The finish eye should be moved to the 60 meter mark.
The Event: Run the same as the 30 meter. Typically the athletes only take two attempts at this event, with the best of two counting.

3. 100 Meters Sprint:
Set up: The finish eye should be moved to the 100 meter mark.
The Event: Run the same as the 30 meter. Typically the athletes only take one attempt at this event.

Note: The three sprint times can be recorded within one sprint, if preferred.

4. Vertical Jump:
Set up: The vertical jump is simply the difference between a standing reach and a jumping reach measured in inches. It is best if administered with a "Vertec," but can also be done against a wall with a tape measure.
The Event: The athlete jumps straight up from a stationery position. The best of three attempts is scored.

5. Five Consecutive Hops:
Set up: The tape is laid out along the track to about 25 meters. The "O" of the tape should be on the front of a "toe line."
The Event: The athlete is not allowed to cross the "toe line" prior to the start. The competitor takes five two legged plyometric hops. They are encouraged to jump quickly. No shuffle steps are allowed. The first time an athlete shuffles, he will be allowed to take another attempt without penalty. The second time the round counts as an attempt but is not scored. Jump distance is measured in meters to the athlete's heel. Again all three jumps should be recorded and the longest is scored.

6. Shot Put Throw:
Set up: If possible the athletes should be able to stand with their feet against a rigid support such as the outside edge of a shot put ring. The area immediately in front of the athlete should be clear and offer as soft a landing for the athlete as possible. The athletes should be given several practice attempts. The tape can be left out, safely off to the side, so that the competitiors get an idea of their throw lengths.
The Event: The shot is thrown forward from between the legs. The athletes take three throws. The results of all attempts should be recorded in meters. The best of the three attempts is scored.

MENS
6 ITEM POINTS SHEET

COACH MAIORCA

Passing Scores:
Drivers: 675
Pushers: 750

Pts.	30 (M)	60 (M)	100 (M)	V. (JUMP)	5 (HOPS)	Wt. (TOSS)
175	3.30	6.20	10.20	42.25	18.25	18.25
174	3.31	6.23	10.23	42.00	18.20	18.20
173	3.32	6.26	10.26	41.75	18.15	18.15
172	3.33	6.29	10.29	41.50	18.10	18.10
171	3.34	6.32	10.32	41.25	18.05	18.05
170	3.35	6.35	10.35	41.00	18.00	18.00
169	3.36	6.38	10.38	40.75	17.95	17.95
168	3.37	6.41	10.41	40.50	17.90	17.90
167	3.38	6.44	10.44	40.25	17.85	17.85
166	3.39	6.47	10.47	40.00	17.80	17.80
165	3.40	6.50	10.50	39.75	17.75	17.75
164	3.41	6.51	10.52	39.50	17.70	17.70
163	3.42	6.52	10.54	39.25	17.65	17.65
162	3.43	6.53	10.56	39.00	17.60	17.60
161	3.44	6.54	10.58	38.75	17.55	17.55
160	3.45	6.55	10.60	38.50	17.50	17.50
159	3.46	6.56	10.62	38.25	17.45	17.45
158	3.47	6.57	10.64	38.00	17.40	17.40
157	3.48	6.58	10.66	37.75	17.35	17.35
156	3.49	6.59	10.68	37.50	17.30	17.30
155	3.50	6.60	10.70	37.25	17.25	17.25
154	3.51	6.61	10.72	37.00	17.20	17.20
153	3.52	6.62	10.74	36.75	17.15	17.15
152	3.53	6.63	10.76	36.50	17.10	17.10
151	3.54	6.64	10.78	36.25	17.05	17.05
150	3.55	6.65	10.80	36.00	17.00	17.00
149	3.56	6.66	10.82	35.75	16.95	16.95
148	3.57	6.67	10.84	35.50	16.90	16.90
147	3.58	6.68	10.86	35.25	16.85	16.85
146	3.59	6.69	10.88	35.00	16.80	16.80
145	3.60	6.70	10.90	34.75	16.75	16.75
144	3.61	6.71	10.92	34.50	16.70	16.70
143	3.62	6.72	10.94	34.25	16.65	16.65
142	3.63	6.73	10.96	34.00	16.60	16.60
141	3.64	6.74	10.98	33.75	16.55	16.55
140	3.65	6.75	11.00	33.50	16.50	16.50
139	3.66	6.76	11.02	33.25	16.45	16.45
138	3.67	6.77	11.04	33.00	16.40	16.40
137	3.68	6.78	11.06	32.75	16.35	16.35
136	3.69	6.79	11.08	32.50	16.30	16.30
135	3.70	6.80	11.10	32.25	16.25	16.25
134	3.71	6.81	11.12	32.00	16.20	16.20
133	3.72	6.82	11.14	31.75	16.15	16.15
132	3.73	6.83	11.16	31.50	16.10	16.10
131	3.74	6.84	11.18	31.25	16.05	16.05
130	3.75	6.85	11.20	31.00	16.00	16.00
129	3.76	6.86	11.22	30.75	15.95	15.95
128	3.77	6.87	11.24	30.50	15.90	15.90
127	3.78	6.88	11.26	30.25	15.85	15.85
126	3.79	6.89	11.28	30.00	15.80	15.80
125	3.80	6.90	11.30	29.75	15.75	15.75
124	3.81	6.91	11.32	29.50	15.70	15.70
123	3.82	6.92	11.34	29.25	15.65	15.65
122	3.83	6.93	11.36	29.00	15.60	15.60
121	3.84	6.94	11.38	28.75	15.55	15.55
120	3.85	6.95	11.40	28.50	15.50	15.50
119	3.86	6.96	11.42	28.25	15.45	15.45
118	3.87	6.97	11.44	28.00	15.40	15.40
117	3.88	6.98	11.46	27.75	15.35	15.35

Pts.	30 (M)	60 (M)	100 (M)	V. (JUMP)	5 (HOPS)	Wt. (TOSS)
116	3.89	6.99	11.48	27.50	15.30	15.30
115	3.90	7.00	11.50	27.25	15.25	15.25
114	3.91	7.01	11.52	27.00	15.20	15.20
113	3.92	7.02	11.54	26.75	15.15	15.15
112	3.93	7.03	11.56	26.50	15.10	15.10
111	3.94	7.04	11.58	26.25	15.05	15.05
110	3.95	7.05	11.60	26.00	15.00	15.00
109	3.96	7.06	11.62	25.75	14.95	14.95
108	3.97	7.07	11.64	25.50	14.90	14.90
107	3.98	7.08	11.66	25.25	14.85	14.85
106	3.99	7.09	11.68	25.00	14.80	14.80
105	4.00	7.10	11.70	24.75	14.75	14.75
104	4.01	7.11	11.72	24.50	14.70	14.70
103	4.02	7.12	11.74	24.25	14.65	14.65
102	4.03	7.13	11.76	24.00	14.60	14.60
101	4.04	7.14	11.78	23.75	14.55	14.55
100	4.05	7.15	11.80	23.50	14.50	14.50
99	4.06	7.16	11.82	23.25	14.45	14.45
98	4.07	7.17	11.84	23.00	14.40	14.40
97	4.08	7.18	11.86	22.75	14.35	14.35
96	4.09	7.19	11.88	22.50	14.30	14.30
95	4.10	7.20	11.90	22.25	14.25	14.25
94	4.11	7.21	11.92	22.00	14.20	14.20
93	4.12	7.22	11.94	21.75	14.15	14.15
92	4.13	7.23	11.96	21.50	14.10	14.10
91	4.14	7.24	11.98	21.25	14.05	14.05
90	4.15	7.25	12.00	21.00	14.00	14.00
89	4.16	7.26	12.02	20.75	13.95	13.95
88	4.17	7.27	12.04	20.50	13.90	13.90
87	4.18	7.28	12.06	20.25	13.85	13.85
86	4.19	7.29	12.08	20.00	13.80	13.80
85	4.20	7.30	12.10	19.75	13.75	13.75
84	4.21	7.31	12.12	19.50	13.70	13.70
83	4.22	7.32	12.14	19.25	13.65	13.65
82	4.23	7.33	12.16	19.00	13.60	13.60
81	4.24	7.34	12.18	18.75	13.55	13.55
80	4.25	7.35	12.20	18.50	13.50	13.50
79	4.26	7.36	12.22	18.25	13.45	13.45
78	4.27	7.37	12.24	18.00	13.40	13.40
77	4.28	7.38	12.26	17.75	13.35	13.35
76	4.29	7.39	12.28	17.50	13.30	13.30
75	4.30	7.40	12.30	17.25	13.25	13.25
74	4.31	7.41	12.32	17.00	13.20	13.20
73	4.32	7.42	12.34	16.75	13.15	13.15
72	4.33	7.43	12.36	16.50	13.10	13.10
71	4.34	7.44	12.38	16.25	13.05	13.05
70	4.35	7.45	12.40	16.00	13.00	13.00
69	4.36	7.46	12.42	15.75	12.95	12.95
68	4.37	7.47	12.44	15.50	12.90	12.90
67	4.38	7.48	12.46	15.25	12.85	12.85
66	4.39	7.49	12.48	15.00	12.80	12.80
65	4.40	7.50	12.50	14.75	12.75	12.75
64	4.41	7.51	12.52	14.50	12.70	12.70
63	4.42	7.52	12.54	14.25	12.65	12.65
62	4.43	7.53	12.56	14.00	12.60	12.60
61	4.44	7.54	12.58	13.75	12.55	12.55
60	4.45	7.55	12.60	13.50	12.50	12.50
59	4.46	7.56	12.62	13.25	12.45	12.45
58	4.47	7.57	12.64	13.00	12.40	12.40

Pts.	30 (M)	60 (M)	100 (M)	V. (JUMP)	5 (HOPS)	Wt. (TOSS)
57	4.48	7.58	12.66	12.75	12.35	12.35
56	4.49	7.59	12.68	12.50	12.30	12.30
55	4.50	7.60	12.70	12.25	12.25	12.25
54	4.51	7.61	12.72	12.00	12.20	12.20
53	4.52	7.62	12.74	11.75	12.15	12.15
52	4.53	7.63	12.76	11.50	12.10	12.10
51	4.54	7.64	12.78	11.25	12.05	12.05
50	4.55	7.65	12.80	11.00	12.00	12.00
49	4.56	7.66	12.82	10.75	11.95	11.95
48	4.57	7.87	12.84	10.50	11.90	11.90
47	4.58	7.68	12.86	10.25	11.85	11.85
46	4.59	7.69	12.88	10.00	11.80	11.80
45	4.60	7.70	12.90	9.75	11.75	11.75
44	4.61	7.71	12.92	9.50	11.70	11.70
43	4.62	7.72	12.94	9.25	11.65	11.65
42	4.63	7.73	12.96	9.00	11.60	11.60
41	4.64	7.74	12.98	8.75	11.55	11.55
40	4.65	7.75	13.00	8.50	11.50	11.50
39	4.66	7.76	13.02	8.25	11.45	11.45
38	4.67	7.77	13.04	8.00	11.40	11.40
37	4.68	7.78	13.06	7.75	11.35	11.35
36	4.69	7.79	13.08	7.50	11.30	11.30
35	4.70	7.80	13.10	7.25	11.25	11.25
34	4.71	7.81	13.12	7.00	11.20	11.20
33	4.72	7.82	13.14	6.75	11.15	11.15
32	4.73	7.83	13.16	6.50	11.10	11.10
31	4.74	7.84	13.18	6.25	11.05	11.05
30	4.75	7.85	13.20	6.00	11.00	11.00
29	4.76	7.86	13.22	5.75	10.95	10.95
28	4.77	7.87	13.24	5.50	10.90	10.90
27	4.78	7.88	13.26	5.25	10.85	10.85
26	4.79	7.89	13.28	5.00	10.80	10.80
25	4.80	7.90	13.30	4.75	10.75	10.75
24	4.81	7.91	13.32	4.50	10.70	10.70
23	4.82	7.92	13.34	4.25	10.65	10.65
22	4.83	7.93	13.36	4.00	10.60	10.60
21	4.84	7.94	13.38	3.75	10.55	10.55
20	4.85	7.95	13.40	3.50	10.50	10.50
19	4.86	7.96	13.42	3.25	10.45	10.45
18	4.87	7.97	13.44	3.00	10.40	10.40
17	4.88	7.98	13.46	2.75	10.35	10.35
16	4.89	7.99	13.48	2.50	10.30	10.30
15	4.90	8.00	13.50	2.25	10.25	10.25
14	4.91	8.01	13.52	2.00	10.20	10.20
13	4.92	8.02	13.54	1.75	10.15	10.15
12	4.93	8.03	13.56	1.50	10.10	10.10
11	4.94	8.04	13.58	1.25	10.05	10.05
10	4.95	8.05	13.60	1.00	10.00	10.00
9	4.96	8.06	13.62	0.75	9.95	9.95
8	4.97	8.07	13.64	0.50	9.90	9.90
7	4.98	8.08	13.66	0.25	9.85	9.85
6	4.99	8.09	13.68	0.00	9.80	9.80
5			13.70		9.75	9.75
4	5.01	8.11	13.72		9.70	9.70
3	5.02	8.12	13.74		9.65	9.65
2	5.03	8.13	13.76		9.60	9.60
1	5.04	8.14	13.78		9.55	9.55
0	5.05	8.15	13.80		9.50	9.50

The Domestic Program

If you cannot score the minimum 750 points on the six-item test or you were not selected to the U.S. National Team, you still may qualify for the USBSF's domestic program in Lake Placid and Park City.

The domestic program was developed to help athletes further their skills so that they can qualify for the U.S. National Team in the future. Selection to the domestic program is limited and will be based on:

- Your six-item test scores
- Your National Push Sled Championship results.

As a Recreational Participant

You may make your plans to travel to Lake Placid or Park City during the domestic sliding season. You will need to apply for a track pass through the offices of the USBSF at least ten days prior to your arrival.

You must also make the Domestic Program Director for the track aware of the dates of your stay. Many of the domestic drivers need push athletes to complete their teams during their training at the tracks. Unfortunately, there is no guarantee that you will get to slide.

To Become a Driver

Unlike a push athlete, a driver must have years of experience in bobsledding to become competitive. Not only is a driver responsible for his own safety and that of his crew, but the driver also leads his team in the complicated preparation of the sled. Furthermore, a driver must be able to excel at the start with the same strength and speed as his pushers. Although many drivers begin in bobsledding as push athletes, there are exceptions to this rule.

In order to qualify as a *recreational driver*, you must:

- Participate in a USBSF Driver's School, which is offered occasionally during the season at both Lake Placid and Park City.
- Train at the Lake Placid or Park City tracks and gain your mile driver's license.

How to Make the Women's Team

It is highly recommended that you study the fundamentals mentioned in the previous section on the U.S. Men's Bobsled Team. In order to be successful, both male and female sliders must possess exceptional mental aptitude and physical strength. All interested athletes are urged to contact the USBSF for further information.

The Basics

To qualify for the team you must:

- Be at least 18 years of age and in good physical condition.
- Be a member of the USBSF by paying the annual fee and completing the Athlete Membership Application, as well as the Physical Form and Proof of Insurance card.
- Sign and accept the Athlete's Contract, Code of Conduct, and Women's Bobsled Criteria Form.
- Be available to compete for the entire bobsled season.

National Women's Team Program

To join the National Women's Team Program, you must:

- Train for and take the USBSF-administered six-item test (see the Men's Team section for more information).
- Participate in the National Push Sled Competition.
- Attend a training camp, including push clinics, competition, and a three-item strength test (squat, power clean, and bench press).

Women's Domestic Team

Athletes who do not qualify for the National Women's Team, either because they did not score 600 points on the six-item test or because they failed to meet other criteria, may still qualify for the Women's Team Domestic Program. This program seeks to develop participants' skills so that they will make the National Team in the future.

6

Athlete Training

Bobsledding is a sport that requires both explosive upper body strength and fast leg speed, combined with keen hand-eye coordination. In addition to a generalized aerobic workout program, it is recommended that an athlete consult with a qualified coach or trainer. This consultation will provide a solid, individually tailored basis for maximizing training performance.

What It Takes to Be a Bobsledder

Bobsled athletes can emerge from a variety of athletic backgrounds. Frequently, they are crossover athletes from football and track and field. However, the only real requirement for becoming a bobsled athlete is speed combined with strength and agility. Any athlete can learn to drive or push a bobsled, but U.S. Bobsled Team members must pass a six-item physical test. The athletes are then placed on teams by the coaches and drivers according to ability levels. Very often, drivers own their own bobsleds. This gives them more freedom to choose teams and compete on a variety of levels. Typically, a bobsled costs $5,000 or more, depending on its age and design.

Each athlete on the team has a different responsibility. A two-man sled requires a driver and a brakeman. A four-man sled needs a driver, two side-pushers, and a brakeman. Bobsledding is a team sport, so each member has equal responsibility in the push as well as the ride. The driver, however, must have great hand-eye coordination to ensure that the sled and his teammates make a safe trip down the icy chute. This is one sport that definitely requires nerves of steel, as the sled often rides at high speeds on the brink of a crash.

The Motivational Factor—Mental Energy

The common denominator in all successful bobsledders is the desire to control their own destiny. A slider must stay in control of something that is basically out of control. Sliders must be open to opportunity and cannot be afraid to try something new, even though it may be dangerous.

In addition to fostering teamwork and camaraderie, the athletes focus on their individual responsibilities with concentration and dedication. During nearly waking moment, they are trying to increase their knowledge of the sport—seeking better training results, memorizing a track's lines, mastering the mechanics of how a bobsled operates. The athletes must learn to be tenacious and agile, and to develop a winning mix of confidence and modesty. The key for any athlete is to believe in oneself and never give up.

The average person watching a bobsled or car race tends to think that the best driver is the one with more courage or the one who is crazier than the others. The truth is: the best drivers are the ones who are the most focused. Once the team has pushed as hard as possible and hopped into the fast-moving sled, it is only the driver who sees the course. Behind the driver sit the pushers, curled up with their heads tucked low to minimize wind resistance. Their fate is now in the hands of the driver.

The character of a good driver is as compelling as the force of gravity felt in the curves and the whiplash felt in a crash. In order to avoid a crash, the driver must know the track well enough so that navigating becomes basic instinct. In the time it takes to think about a curve, the sled has already gone through it. Therefore, the driver must pre-visualize his moves because of the sled's speed and constantly changing attitude.

Each banked turn poses a different problem. To deal with this, athletes use a learning skill called *visualization*. At each venue, every bobsledder walks the track—stopping at each curve, creating a mental picture so detailed that the athlete is able to "see" the track, with eyes closed, with precision down to the inch. A bobsled driver walking a previously studied course will face downhill, eyes closed, arms out in front, and pantomime the minute hand movements required as he mentally steers into and out of the turn.

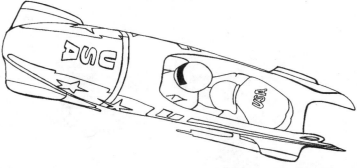

Illus. by Frank Posluszny

The pushers must walk the track as well. Despite riding blind, they must know precisely at each moment where they are on the track. They must be able to sense when the sled is entering a turn so that they can shift their weight in the appropriate direction. If the riders are being tossed about from side to side, the sled loses forward momentum, which costs time.

Although the process of visualization may seem difficult or tedious, it is really similar to learning any new task. Once you have taken the time to learn the basics, the actions required to control the sled become much clearer. The task is no longer a confusing blur, but rather something that can be accomplished if it is broken down into segments and learned as a series of individual steps. First-time bobsled drivers don't learn by starting at the top of the track. They start a third or halfway up the course to get the feel of how to steer a sled at slower speeds.

Once an athlete has learned the fundamentals of driving, it is time to race. Right before the beginning of the push-start, the driver will do a pre-race focus that in essence empties his mind and resets his mental process to act on instinct. He may visualize a problem curve, but then turns his attention back to the start.

Nancy Pierpoint
Brian Shimer walks the track in St. Moritz.

Once the ballet of brute force called a push-start is over, the driver must now employ the hand-eye dexterity of a surgeon. In a sport where no more than one one-hundredth of a second often separates one sled from another, nothing less than total concentration will do. The perfect line the driver seeks represents a delicate balance of gravity and minute steering moves. Every time the driver steers the slightest bit, a runner cuts into the ice and slows the sled's momentum. However, if the driver doesn't steer, the sled is bound to drift too high into a curve and crash. The driver who steers the least has the best chance of a winning time.

Training Principles

It is important for both athlete and coach to understand the fundamentals of recovery, balance, and technique in outlining a sledder's training program.

In order for athletic performance to improve, a *recovery* phase must follow a hard training session. The body's natural response to hard training is to rebuild fatigued muscles during this recovery time so that they are stronger than before. The length of the recovery phase varies depending on the amount of stress placed on the body during training. It is important to schedule rest and recovery periods during training because a strained athlete makes for a poor athlete. The amount of strenuous physical labor a young person can handle varies depending on the individual's age, physical development, training background, and attitude. These factors must be considered when arranging a training program for a sport as intensive as bobsledding.

A bobsledder's competitive performance actually involves a delicate sequential balance of different body movements. Therefore, *balance* in training is essential and needs to be carefully planned. Bobsled races are rarely won by a solid push-start alone, although they can be lost by a poor one. The push-start is the most critical part of a sledder's actions. Within a few short seconds, the team members use the powerful and explosive strength of their legs and upper body to propel themselves and a sled weighing several hundred pounds from a standing start. While they push, they must also move from a dead-start to a running-push position. Working in coordination, the athletes then must load themselves into the sled and assume their assigned race positions—all while maintaining their forward momentum.

Balanced training requires a long-term commitment and complete dedication. To become a skilled bobsledder, an athlete must seek a compromise between power and endurance training. To qualify for the six-item test and maintain team status, a sledder's objective must be to score the maximum number of possible points. All athletes have "off" days, when their strengths may become weaknesses. The advantage in bobsledding is that both team qualification and winning in competition depend on a combined total score. Therefore, a mistake or weakness in one area can be offset by an outstanding performance in another. The first priority in training, then, should be to strive for dependability and confidence as a whole, even though some areas may be weaker than others.

Learning sound *technique* also is a key concern for athletes who are just beginning the training process. Perfect technique does not happen naturally. It is something that is taught and learned with experience. As experience grows, a bobsledder's speed, power, and endurance will increase. Many potential sledders, including the National Football League's Herschel Walker and Willie Gault and Olympic hurdles champ Edwin Moses, have hampered team performance simply by failing to devote the time needed to learn correct execution. While bobsledding borrows principles from other sports such as football and track, it is the combination of those principles that makes the athlete's job harder and provides the most satisfaction once mastered. If an athlete's form is not biomechanically sound, it will have to be unlearned, then relearned. The key for serious athletes is to keep returning, learning, and repeating until a suitable form is established.

Training Fundamentals

A feasible bobsled training program includes the following six components: technique, speed, speed endurance, strength training, endurance training, and flexibility training.

Technique

Simply put, the goal is to find an easy, mechanically sound technique best suited to the athlete. The greatest emphasis on developing a technique should come in a sledder's earlier years, when motor patterns are developing.

Speed

Much of a bobsledder's performance is directly related to speed. Speed training can be accomplished year-round.

The intensity of drills and workouts should increase during the sledding season and in preparation for competitions. A series of sprints over 30, 60, and 100 meters is a common exercise routine. Allow adequate rest between sprints. Drills to maintain sprint form and practice start positions are also critical.

Speed Endurance

The emphasis here is to maintain developed speed over a longer distance with good sprint form and proper body carriage. Various combinations of runs over 100 meters may be used to train.

Hans Kummer

Men's and women's teams taking the six-item test in Lake Placid, NY

Strength Training

A bobsledder's early career should emphasize a general strength-training program using traditional weightlifting exercises. Olympic lifts such as the snatch and the clean and jerk can be used, along with such power lifts as the bench press and half-squat. These exercises increase the body's overall strength. A beginning slider may choose to limit his or her activity to a circuit on a Universal Gym or other similar equipment.

Specific strength training is aimed at developing power in the "explosion" of a standing start, running, and jumping. Such training uses dynamic exercises that attempt to imitate the movements executed during a push-start. Medicine ball drills, jumping, bounding, and hopping are just a few of the possible workouts.

General strength training takes precedence over specific training in an athlete's early career. Once a proficiency level in most activities is reached, strength training can be split between general and specific programs. The intended goal of weightlifting is to increase strength, not build bulk. Strength training must work in tandem with technique workouts.

Remember: never lift alone. Always lift with a spotter, friend, or another athlete. Never overexert yourself. When working with weights, it's better to be safe than sorry.

Endurance Training

This training phase develops an aerobic base that enables the athlete to acquire the stamina and endurance required for bobsled competition. Endurance training can be accomplished in the off-season by frequently running for 20 to 30 minutes. This should be combined with a varied aerobic workout program, two to three times a week. During the competitive season, several long-distance, paced runs are recommended for conditioning and esteem building.

Flexibility Training

Every workout should be preceded by a 15- to 20-minute stretching session. Often overlooked, this practice is an important part of the training process. Not only does it help prevent injuries, but it also improves technique by allowing the body a greater range of motion.

For many people, running is the best and most convenient form of exercise. Occasionally, however, your legs need a break. When your legs feel achy or sluggish, try inline skating. Researchers at the University of Massachusetts at Amherst have found that inline skating causes significantly less impact shock to the body than running does. The study suggests that the knees, hips, and spine benefit most from an occasional break from running.

Integrate Your Training Regimen

To help you incorporate cross-training into your running program, here are some examples of different sports and their equivalent times or distances for running.

A. A two-hour bike ride = a 30–45 minute "easy" run
B. Two hours of cross-country skiing = a ten-mile run
C. A 1.5-mile swim = a six-mile run
D. Two miles of rowing = a one-mile run
E. A 10K inline skate = a 5K run

Training Cycles

Some athletes prefer to arrange their workout schedules in cycles—including 7-day, 14-day, or 21-day plans. These plans have built-in flexibility and will vary in intensity depending on in-season or off-season activities. In-season work generally focuses on refining speed, maintaining speed endurance, and perfecting technique. Off-season activities work more with strength and endurance.

Training Tips

The experience, ability, and interest of a 15-year-old who is seriously committed to the sport will differ greatly from those of a 22-year-old. However, their basic goals are the same: to train well and compete to the best of their abilities in future bobsled races. Here are a few tips to prevent injury and keep a positive outlook during the heavy demands of bobsled training:

• Have at least one training partner. Partners can offer advice, support, competition, and sympathy and make the effort more fun.

• Plan a sufficient amount of rest or easy time. Insufficient or no rest only leads to injuries.

• If you can, vary your workout sites. Given the heavy physical demands of bobsledding, it's easy to fall into a tedious routine. Working out at different sites can help to avoid this.

• Don't ignore your weak areas and don't be afraid to experiment.

• On any given training day, do sprint and technique work when you are fresh, before a speed endurance exercise. Power training and endurance work should be done at the end of the session. Doing them first will only lead to injuries.

• If you have established a training cycle, technique work should follow a rest or easy training day. Speed and speed endurance should be placed in the middle of the cycle, and endurance and strength workouts placed at the end.

• If you become tired, stop. It is better to be conservative and let less be more. Countless injuries have happened when athletes try to push "just one more" repetition or try to run "just one more" lap. Injuries can harm or end a career. Use your common sense and set a predetermined number of efforts. Do them and then stop.

Chapter Acknowledgments

For the detailed information on training I am greatly indebted to earlier Guides in the USOC Sports Series, particularly the "Decathlon Training" chapter in *A Basic Guide to Decathlon,* written by Dr. Frank Zarnowski.

7

Nutrition and Health

An athlete's performance is greatly influenced by diet. Eating the right amounts of the right kinds of food will help ensure maximum results. The "Zone" diet of 40 percent carbohydrates, 30 percent protein, and 30 percent fat is generally recommended for most athletes during both training and competition. Athletes needing a higher energy intake for increased performance may consider a diet of 70 percent carbohydrates, 20 percent protein, and 10 percent fat.

Elements of Nutrition

Carbohydrates are the starches and sugars found in grains (pasta, rice, bread, cereal products), fruits and vegetables, and milk and dairy products, as well as in many of the over-the-counter sports drinks and nutritional supplements available today. Some experts believe that an equal mix of complex and simple carbohydrates is the key to fueling long workouts.

To find the ratio of complex-to-simple carbohydrates in food, subtract the grams of sugar (simple carbohydrates) from the total carbohydrates. This will give you the amount of complex carbohydrates, which should be nearly equal to the amount of simple carbohydrates for an effective training diet.

Proteins are known as the "building blocks" of the body. Proteins aid in the growth process, help the digestive process, and assist in fighting infection and repairing damaged cells. Milk and dairy products, meats, fish, eggs, and nuts are all significant sources of protein.

Fats are food energy in a concentrated form. They help build and maintain body tissue and contain the fat-soluble vitamins A, D, E, and K. Unsaturated fats are found in nuts and many vegetable oils. Saturated fats can be found in milk and many dairy products, red meat, and whole eggs. Fat should typically be no more than 10–20 percent of an athlete's food consumption during peak training and competition. Some athletes choose to follow a mainly vegetarian diet that is low in fat and high in carbohydrates and plant proteins.

An athlete also needs a wide variety of vitamins, minerals, and fiber to round out the diet. By eating a wide range of healthy foods and beverages, with the correct proportions of nutrients, athletes can obtain the vitamins, minerals, and energy their bodies demand. A varied diet usually meets these requirements, but a quality multi-vitamin/multi-mineral supplement is also recommended.

The more active you are, the more energy you need. Bobsledders need more energy than the average person and generally use 5,000 calories or more per day. Nutritional research indicates that the needed extra energy should come from increasing carbohydrate intake rather than additional fat or protein.

Your total energy consumption should consistently be increased to replace the energy drained during training. Sledders should always monitor their food intake, body weight, and percentage of body fat to maintain optimum performance. Nutritionally speaking, bobsledding is both a power and an endurance sport, so increased energy is a critical aspect.

Fluid intake is an essential element of nutrition. Athletes need to drink extra water. All body cells contain water. In fact, water

A Guide to Daily Food Choices

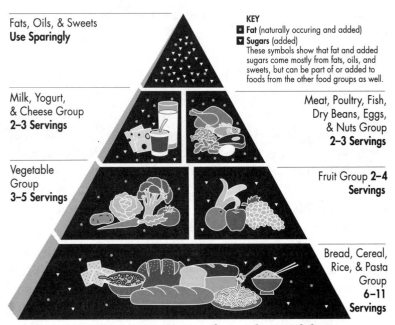

Fats, Oils, & Sweets
Use Sparingly

KEY
■ **Fat** (naturally occuring and added)
▼ **Sugars** (added)
These symbols show that fat and added sugars come mostly from fats, oils, and sweets, but can be part of or added to foods from the other food groups as well.

Milk, Yogurt,
& Cheese Group
2–3 Servings

Meat, Poultry, Fish,
Dry Beans, Eggs,
& Nuts Group
2–3 Servings

Vegetable
Group
3–5 Servings

Fruit Group **2–4
Servings**

Bread, Cereal,
Rice, & Pasta
Group
**6–11
Servings**

Source: U.S. Department of Agriculture and the
U.S. Department of Health and Human Services

accounts for 60 percent of your body weight. Water transports nutrients, maintains blood volume, and helps cool the body. Dehydration, the loss of body fluid, causes the body to overheat and can impair performance. Athletes should not wait until they feel thirsty to drink. Drinking more than you think you should *before* you feel thirsty ensures endurance during training and competition.

Although some athletes enjoy an occasional alcoholic beverage, consuming alcohol does not prevent dehydration. In fact, it increases rather than decreases dehydration. Alcohol is a diuretic: it increases urine formation, so that slightly more body fluid is lost as urine than is consumed in the beverage. Under no circumstances should a bobsled athlete have alcohol in any form during training or competition.

Nutritional Supplements

You should be suspicious of any supplement that claims amazing results. Most nutritional research does not support those claims. If you take such supplements, be aware that you do so at your own risk, and that such supplements are not endorsed by the USOC.

Typical athletes eating an adequate diet will find little need for supplements. However, if the athlete has a natural deficiency or if the workload is abnormally high, a supplement may be advisable. A young athlete concerned about a possible nutritional deficiency should consult a physician.

Good Health Practices

Bobsledders of any age, particularly those with recognized talents, are exposed to an extensive array of influences. For many, the desire to give in to external or internal pressures creates habits that can deviate from a healthy lifestyle and can ultimately jeopardize the athlete's health and career.

Alcohol and Drugs

For many adult Americans, drinking an alcoholic beverage is a routine part of life, and they partake in a responsible manner. Many of the world's bobsledding venues are in European countries that view "having a few pints at the local pub" as a social and celebratory way of life. For bobsled athletes, the question of what and what not to drink weighs heavily in their social lives. As mentioned previously, alcohol is a dehydrating substance as well as a depressant.

Because of social pressures, many young people drink immoderately. The risks associated with excessive alcohol consumption, including drunk-driving accidents, are high. If an athlete avoids alcohol during training and competition and drinks in moderation at other times, the impact on a bobsledding career likely will be negligible. The same cannot be said for the use of any recreational drugs. There is no place in any sport for these unlawful substances. Remember that as an American bobsledding athlete, you are representing not just yourself, your family, and your team, but also your country. Breaking the law by taking drugs does irreparable damage on many different levels.

Anabolic Steroids

The use of anabolic-androgenic steroids (AAS) became prominent in the U.S. Mid-Atlantic weightlifting community in the late 1950s and early 1960s. Steroid drugs are taken to boost athletic performance and stimulate muscle development. Evidence suggests that both are accomplished in a short period of time, but with a heavy price paid on long-term health. The negative consequences of steroid use easily outnumber the possible benefits of performance enhancement.

The use of AAS in young boys can result in hair loss, overdeveloped breasts, yellowing of the eyes, acne, and stunted body growth. Research has revealed that the use of anabolic steroids produces psychological effects that include extreme mood swings, irritability, delusions, jealousy, and impaired judgment.

It should be noted that steroid use in the U.S. bobsled community is virtually nonexistent. Frequent drug testing, both in and out of competition, ensures that athletes are not using illegal substances. Nevertheless, a large number of young male non-athletes do use the drugs to "bulk up." It is estimated that sales of illegal steroids in the U.S. now exceed $400 million annually. The majority of sales are from mail order companies or gyms that secretly "prescribe" them. Health problems connected with steroid use already are becoming more prevalent, and America will pay the price as today's young people grow older.

Tobacco

The damage to an athlete's lungs from smoking and the effects of tobacco as a cancer-causing agent are substantial and undeniable. Not only is tobacco an addictive drug, but it also steadily reduces the lung capacity of even the strongest young athletes. Since bobsledding is both a power sport and an endurance sport, sledders who intend to make it a career should abstain from smoking.

Surprisingly, as the number of U.S. smokers declines, the number of people taking up smokeless tobacco is rising. Like smoking cigarettes, using smokeless tobacco is addictive. Smokeless tobacco has been linked to mouth cancers. Pouch tobacco has a typical sugar content of 35 percent. Continually subjecting your teeth to sugar greatly increases the risk of cavities, gum disease, and loss of teeth.

Chapter Acknowledgments

I am greatly indebted to earlier Guides in the USOC Sports Series for their frank and detailed information, particularly the nutrition chapter in *A Basic Guide to Decathlon,* written by Dr. Frank Zarnowski.

8

First Aid

Bobsledding safety cannot be overemphasized. No one ever wants to see an athlete get hurt. Many bobsledding injuries can be avoided through a proper medical examination, correct flexibility training, and appropriate physical conditioning. Since all athletes do get bumps and bruises—and, occasionally, more serious injuries—here are a few precautions to keep in mind at practices and competitions:

- Wear the right clothes for practice sessions.
- Leave any jewelry—watches, rings, earrings, etc.—in your locker or in a duffel bag. This rule applies to boys as well as girls.
- Stow equipment in a safe place, where it won't interfere with athletes who are warming up, practicing, or competing.
- Go through a warmup session and do stretching exercises before the practice begins. This prevents muscle strains and aches and pains.
- Skip a practice if you are not feeling well. Recovery will be quicker than if you had practiced or competed while under the weather.
- Drink plenty of water. Dehydration can occur quickly. Don't wait until you are thirsty to get a drink. Some coaches recommended sports drinks and think they are useful, but water is just as good, if not better.

The First Aid Kit

Injuries go hand-in-hand with sports. It's wise to know what to do to handle the inevitable bumps, bruises, and scrapes, along with more serious injuries. A well-stocked first aid kit should include:

- Adhesive bandages in different shapes and sizes
- Adhesive tape in different sizes
- Ammonia caps for dizziness
- Antiseptic soap for washing a wound area
- Antiseptic solution for minor scrapes
- Aspirin, or its equivalent, for simple headaches.
  (Remember: For youth teams, no medication should be given without written permission from a doctor or guardian, signed and dated, authorizing the disbursement of aspirin or other medication.)
- Blanket to cover an injured athlete, since warmth reduces the risk of shock
- Cold packs
- Disposable towels
- Elastic wraps of various sizes
- Eyewash solution
- Gauze pads
- Hank's solution for a knocked-out tooth (trade name Save-A-Tooth®)
- Plastic bottle filled with fresh water
- Scissors and an eyedropper
- Sterile cotton sheets that can be cut to fit
- Tissues and premoistened towelettes
- Tweezers

Remember that Occupational Safety and Health Administration (OSHA) regulations must be followed when disposing of any items that have blood contamination.

It is a good idea to have a list of emergency telephone numbers taped inside the first aid kit, but in a real emergency, dial 911. Be sure to keep some spare change in the first aid kit to use with a pay telephone.

Treating Injuries and Other Problems

Many large competitions have a physician, nurse, or other trained health care professional on hand to take care of any serious injury. However, you should never assume that precautions have been taken. Check in advance to be sure. Always be prepared. Proper planning prevents problems.

In coping with a serious injury, coaches may find the following guidelines helpful:

- Always remain calm. Don't panic or appear flustered. Others around you will take their behavior cues from you.
- Don't try to be a doctor. When in doubt about the severity of an injury, send the athlete to a physician, or let the on-site physician, nurse, or other health care professional make the decision.
- Never move a bobsledder who has a serious injury. Don't try to make the injured person more comfortable by moving the bobsledder away from the competition area or into the locker room. This can make a serious injury worse. Be safe, not sorry, and call in the designated professionals if you have doubts about an injury. Under no circumstances should an unconscious bobsledder be moved. Stay with the athlete until a professional arrives.

Scrapes and Burns

Wash scrapes and burns with an antiseptic cleaning solution and cover with sterile gauze. This is usually all that is needed to promote quick healing of these common injuries.

Cuts

Small cuts need pressure to slow the bleeding. After the bleeding slows, wash the area with an antiseptic solution, cover with sterile gauze taped in place, and continue to apply pressure. Of course, any deep cut or large gash may need stitches, so the injured bobsledder should see a doctor as soon as possible.

Communicable Diseases

Communicable diseases such as boils, athlete's foot, ringworm, and cold sores are common afflictions among athletes. Mouth sores may be treated with over-the-counter medications, but the bobsledder should check with a coach or doctor before using any of these. The best medicine, however, is prevention. Bobsledders should avoid using other people's equipment, and should make sure to keep their own equipment clean.

Muscle Pulls, Sprains, and Bruises

Rest, ice, compression, and elevation (**RICE**) are the steps needed to handle these injuries and are about all you should do in the way of treatment. RICE reduces the swelling of most injuries and helps speed recovery.

After an injury, the coach should have the injured bobsledder stop and rest. Apply ice, compress with an elastic bandage, and elevate the injured arm, leg, knee, or ankle. Ice reduces swelling and pain, and should be left on the injured area until it becomes uncomfortable. When that happens, remove the ice pack and let the injured bobsledder rest for 15 minutes, then reapply. These are the immediate steps to take until a doctor arrives.

Over the next few days, the injury should be treated with two to three 20-minute icing sessions per day at two and one-half hour intervals. This should provide noticeable improvement. Don't overdo the icing; 20 minutes is long enough. In most cases, after two or three days, or when the swelling has been significantly reduced, heat can be applied in the form of warm-water soaks. Fifteen minutes of warm soaking, along with a gradual return to motion, will speed the healing process.

Another approach after two or three days, if the doctor agrees, is to begin motion, strength, and alternative (**MSA**) exercise. The American Institute for Preventive Medicine recommends:

- Motion: Moving the injured area and reestablishing a range of motion.
- Strength: Working to increase the strength of the injured area once any inflammation subsides and the range of motion begins to return.
- Alternative: Regularly performing an alternative exercise that does not stress the injury.

Seek the advice of a sports-medicine professional prior to starting any treatment plan. Specially shaped pads are useful for knee and ankle injuries, and they can be used in combination with ice, compression, and elevation. For a simple bruise, apply an ice pack.

Head Injuries

Blows to the upper part of the head, especially near the eye, can cause bleeding under the skin and result in a black eye. An ice pack applied to the area will reduce the swelling until a doctor can evaluate the injury.

Normally, the eye can wash out most foreign particles because of its ability to produce tears. If this doesn't work, use an eye-cleaning solution to wash out the irritant. Here are a few simple guidelines a bobsledder can follow when dealing with an eye irritant:

- Don't rub the eye or use anything dirty, such as a cloth or a finger, to remove the irritant.

- With clean hands, pull the eyelid forward and down as you look at the floor.
- Flush with eyewash, or use a clean, sterile cloth to remove any particle you see in the eye.

If the foreign object remains, the coach should cover the eye with a clean gauze pad and have the athlete visit a doctor.

Nosebleeds usually don't last very long. A bobsledder with a nosebleed should sit quietly and apply a cold pack to the bridge of the nose, while pinching the nostril at its base.

A knocked-out tooth can be successfully replanted if it is stored and transported properly. The tooth should be placed in a transport container with a solution such as Hank's or Viaspan®, which is available over-the-counter at a drugstore. The coach and all medical personnel at a bobsled competition should be alert to the importance of knowing how to care for a knocked-out tooth.

Fractures and Broken Bones

It is sometimes difficult to distinguish a broken finger from one that is merely jammed. Use a cold pack to control swelling and pain. If there is no improvement within the hour, the finger should be X-rayed.

To safely move a person with an injury to the hand or wrist, follow these steps:

- A finger with a mild swelling can be taped to an adjacent finger.
- An elastic bandage may be gently wrapped around an injured wrist to give the wrist support. Do not wrap heavily, and do not pull the bandage tight.

A fracture or a broken bone can be recognized by some or all of the following:

- A part of the body is bent or twisted out of its normal shape.
- A bone has pierced the skin.
- Swelling is severe and more than the swelling associated with a typical sprain or bruise.
- The hand or foot becomes extremely cold, which may indicate pinching of a major blood vessel.

If the bobsledder has a possible broken leg or arm, the best approach is *not* to move the leg or arm in any manner. A cold pack can be used to lessen the discomfort until medical personnel arrive, and the bobsledder should be kept warm with a blanket. It is important to get prompt medical attention when a fracture occurs.

Remember: Never move a seriously injured bobsledder. Instead, get prompt medical attention or call for emergency aid. Until medical personnel arrive, cover the injured bobsledder with a lightweight blanket, to reduce the risk of shock.

9

The Active Spectator Sport

Recreational sliding rides are offered at bobsled runs at Lake Placid, New York, and Park City, Utah. For a fee, both facilities have winter and summer ride programs available to the general public, weather and track conditions permitting.

Winter Ride Program

Ride a Bobsled

Visitors can now experience the same sensation Olympic athletes feel as they rocket down the track in a bobsled. Both mile and half-mile rides are offered at the two tracks. A professional driver and brakeman accompany passengers. Bobsled passengers are outfitted with special helmets.

If you choose to take part, you will reach speeds approaching 50 mph from the half-mile start and more than 70 mph from the top. You will feel the incredible weight of G forces on your body, pressing you into the bottom of the sled as you fly through the turns. Mile riders will also experience a 180-degree turn just above the half-mile point. Reservations are required for this program.

Hans Kummer

The Bobsled Passenger Ride Program takes off in Park City.

Ice Rocket Rides

The Ice Rocket combines the thrill of bobsledding with the fun and excitement of tubing. Both the Lake Placid and Park City facilities offer this padded four-passenger sled that has no driver or brakeman, but is aerodynamically designed to guide itself down the track. The Ice Rocket reaches speeds in excess of 60 mph.

Summer Ride Program

Ride a Bobsled

Formerly, bobsledding was a sport that could be enjoyed only during the cold winter months. Now summertime visitors to Lake Placid and Park City can experience the thrills of one of winter's most daring sports.

Illus. by
Frank Posluszny

Designed by bobsled authorities, the summer sleds are mounted on rubber wheels. A unique combination of special bearings and braking systems allows bobsledders to pilot their sleds exactly as they would in winter. Maneuvered by professional drivers and brakemen, the summer bobsled trip is nearly identical to the winter ride. Descending from the half-mile start, summer bobsledders will reach speeds of more than 45 mph as they race through the turns into the G force-inducing finish curve.

Observing a Bob Race in Person

Everyone who is interested in the sport should attend a bobsled competition. The sights, sounds, and sensations of a race are a significant part of what makes the sport so interesting—and what makes bobsledding the most popular European winter spectator sport. The breathtaking mountain scenery and silence of a light snowfall set the tone. The surroundings are enlivened by an eclectic mix of languages spoken around every corner. Some fans continue the tradition of ringing cowbells, cheering, and chanting as they root for their favorite teams.

In fact, bobsleigh is so popular in Europe that it rivals NASCAR racing in America in terms of fan attendance, demographics, merchandising, and support for specific athletes. At any given race, you will find fans perusing the work and warmup areas to pick up pointers that will help their own sliding.

Most bobsled tracks have a convenient walkway that winds down the hillside next to the track, providing excellent viewing sites at a variety of different angles. You can obtain the best view by positioning yourself on a catwalk that passes over the track (during training only, since such locations usually are reserved for technical delegates and jury members during competitions) or at a spot at the lower end of a large turn. Both sites allow for maximum viewing of each sled as it enters a turn from the straightaway, races through the turn, and speeds into the next maneuver. If you are taking pictures, remember that you should not use a flash because the quick burst of light may distract or temporarily blind the athletes.

Team performance is determined by calculating the fastest combined aggregate time over four runs (heats) by each team over two consecutive days. The wise spectator should watch for and compare the team's posted push-start time with the finish-line time. A fast start can win a race in which fractions of a second mean the difference between victory and defeat. If you are at the starting gate for the push, watch the athletes use a crossover step (right foot over left foot; left over right) to keep their forward momentum as they get in the sled. This crucial maneuver can make or break the team's chance at a medal, since the bobsledders are pushing the sled about 50 meters in less than five seconds, and can lose their footing or catch their spikes on the sled or another athlete.

Once in the sled, the driver attempts to minimize the number of steering maneuvers. Watch for ice spray—this usually indicates that the pilot is steering too hard into or out of corners and is creating friction between the sled and the track. This inevitably results in a slower finish time. Best results occur when the crew stays as still as possible and the driver lets the sled use gravity to do the work. Drivers try to keep their sleds from rocking side to side when exiting curves. Each driver seeks to maintain the straightest possible line down the course. The sled that appears to slingshot cleanly out of a curve is usually the one that will post the fastest time.

Listen! Most sleds can be heard approaching from a quarter of a mile away because of sled vibrations.

Viewing a Bob Race on Television

The popularity of bobsledding continues to pick up speed and shows no signs of slowing down. With the growth of cable and satellite television services, as well as the explosion of sports coverage worldwide, bobsledding has finally emerged as a popular spectator sport for viewers around the planet. The intense media coverage of recent Olympic events has helped propel the sport.

In fact, bobsledding has been rated as the second most-watched Olympic television event after ice skating. An ongoing commitment to broadcast future Olympic Games by such American networks as CBS, Turner Broadcasting, and NBC should draw tremendous attention from people in all walks of life.

EuroSport airs all the Bobsled World Cup events live and promotes the sport by comparing it to Formula One auto racing. EuroSport's bobsled ratings have been the highest for any sport it broadcasts. Bobsledding also can be seen in North America on ESPN, ESPN2, the Prime Network family of Regional Sports Networks, and CBC in Canada.

John Morgan, whose family name is synonymous with U.S. bobsledding, has become a popular television analyst for international bobsled events. He has covered many of the Olympic Games, as well as the World Cup for ESPN and EuroSport. He served as a commentator in the hit Disney film *Cool Runnings*.

10

Cool Tips

For Athletes

- Do the best you can in each heat, remembering that you are attempting to be the team with the best combined time for each race. Bobsledders compete against themselves to make each run as fast and clean as possible, while keeping a watchful eye on the competition's results.
- The combined score is most important. Winning each single event is not. Because bobsledding runs occur over a period of two consecutive days, competitors have the chance to correct mistakes and keep the team in medal contention.
- Think positive. Carrying frustration or anger from one event to another always leads to clouded judgment and poor results. Even if things are not going as planned, remain in the race and, most important, *finish* the race by giving it 100 percent.
- Be aggressive to the very end. Even if your team had a bad push-start, a smart driver can try compensating with fast and clean steering, which may make up time at the finish line.
- Familiarize yourself with the FIBT Rule Book.
- Many psychological problems, including stress, anxiety, and nervousness, can be resolved by proper organization. Good sleep, nutrition, and workout habits foster physiological and psychological fitness. Remember the Boy Scouts motto: "Always be prepared."

- Bobsledding is more than just a physical competition. It is a test of character and attitude about life. During the 1996–97 World Cup season, bobsled driver Brian Shimer crashed in training for the first race, causing a golf-ball-sized knot between his eyes and bruising his ribs. He rebounded to enjoy an outstanding season—winning six World Cup medals, including three golds, as well as garnering two bronze medals at the World Championships.
- Take pride in the records you set, but remember that the only records you *own* are personal ones. You are only holding world, national, or other records until someone else comes along and breaks them. Someday, someone will. Records are meant to be broken.
- Honor your competitors with your best effort. Expect nothing less than their best, too.
- Be cordial to your competitors and to officials after the competition.

For Coaches

- Have patience. Remember that having a positive and flexible outlook is key.
- Until recently, bobsledding typically has not been a sport of long-term commitment by younger children. As a child's interest evolves, it is the responsibility of the coach to nurture that interest and promote the child's potential.
- Know and enforce the rules.
- Do not expect athletes to set personal records in every aspect of the sport. Potential sledders may be turned off by inappropriate expectations from their coaches.
- Make sure the athlete is fully qualified to handle the physical and psychological pressures of competition. Exaggerating performances and scores on entry blanks may take a position away from someone more deserving. Nothing hurts a team more than an athlete who is obviously not prepared for a particular level of competitive intensity.

- Maintain positive yet realistic expectations regarding how long it takes an athlete to improve and advance to higher competitive levels. Improvement is usually rapid early in an athlete's career but then gradually tapers off.
- Encourage teamwork. As the foundation for group trust evolves, athletes will teach, learn from, and encourage others.
- Offer individualized suggestions and/or assistance for your athletes; this will help inspire trust and confidence. Do not recruit young athletes unless you are willing to foster their strengths and stimulate them to overcome their weaknesses.

For Parents and Other Relatives

- Attend as many events as possible. Support and encouragement from parents, other relatives, and friends are vital factors in improving an athlete's outlook and performance.
- As a parent, it is important to remember the difference between encouragement and pressure. Young sledders may feel undue pressure to perform simply because their parents are watching. It is important for children to know that you will support them regardless of the final outcome.
- Always inspire your child to be fair and nonjudgmental about people or events. As in life, sometimes the greatest lessons come from difficult situations.
- Don't brag. Remember that your child's strengths may be another's weak area. Bragging only serves to undermine the very principles of sportsmanship that you have tried to instill in your child. It can also erode team spirit.

11

Further Reading

If you are interested in additional information on bobsled-related topics, consider reading the following titles:

Bobsleigh History

Triet, Max. *A Centenary of Bobsleighing*. Basel, Switzerland: Swiss Sports Museum, 1990.

Magazines/Newsletters

The Icebreaker, the official newsletter of the U.S. Bobsled and Skeleton Federation, P.O. Box 828, Lake Placid, NY 12946 (three issues per year).

Olympian, c/o U.S. Olympic Committee, One Olympic Plaza, Colorado Springs, CO 80909 (six issues per year).

12

Glossary

Aerobic Literally means "with oxygen." The term refers to sustained exercises, such as jogging or calisthenics, designed to stimulate and strengthen the heart without causing a loss of oxygen to the muscles.

Aerodynamics As applied to racing, the study of airflow and the forces of resistance and pressure that result from the flow of air over, under, and around a moving sled or car.

Anabolic steroids Hormones, particularly testosterone, that promote muscle tissue growth. These have been banned by organizations governing sports. Such organizations periodically test athletes for the presence of anabolic steroids; a positive test result may result in the athlete's being banned from a sport.

Anaerobic Literally means "in the absence of oxygen." The term refers to exercise designed to strengthen the heart while muscles lose oxygen (e.g., sprinting).

Automatic timing Timing accomplished by an electronic device that discriminates within one one-hundredth of a second. Automatic timing is required in order for a record time to be verified.

Bobsled A racing sled with steering ability to control movement of its front runners. Two-man and four-man versions are allowed in competition. Early sleds consisted of two short toboggans joined in tandem. The term originates from the English word *bob*, meaning a hanging object. The second short sled was viewed as hanging from the first. A bobsled may also be referred to as a "bobsleigh."

Chassis roll Describes the up-and-down swaying motion of a vehicle as it travels through corners at high speeds. The side of the vehicle that faces the inside of the turn tends to get lighter and rise upward as it comes through the turn. The proper side-to-side adjustment of the pushers' weight minimizes chassis roll.

Checking Checking occurs when a driver who does not purposely want to steer tugs back on the steering ropes.

Chute The straightaway of a bobrun or racetrack.

Continental championships Single-event bobsled races at a European or a North American venue. The heats are run by teams from their respective continents. A team's combined run time determines medal ranking.

Crew chief   A team leader. Depending on how the team is organized, the crew chief's responsibilities may include anything from maintaining equipment to handling airline and hotel reservations.

Curvature   The slope of a track, particularly at a curve or corner, from the bottom edge of the track to the top lip. "Degree of curvature" refers to the height of the track's slope at its outside edge.

"Doing the   The process of sanding, polishing, and
runners"   subsequently heating a sled's runners in an aggressive and repetitive long stroking motion.

Doping control   Monitoring procedures designed to determine whether the athletes participating in an event are using certain banned substances (steroids, cocaine, heroin, PCP, alcohol, prescription drugs, etc.). As part of doping control, the FIBT and Olympic committees require that sledders undergo frequent drug testing to ensure fairness and safety.

Downforce   The pressure of the air on a sled or car as it races. Downforce is a combination of aerodynamic and centrifugal forces. More downforce means more grip and improved cornering capabilities, but a loss of speed and more drag. Since speed is essential, a sled requires as little downforce as possible.

Drag   A resisting force exerted on a sled or car parallel to its airstream and opposite in direction to its motion. The more aerodynamic a vehicle's body, the lower the drag.

Exiting speed A critical element in achieving a fast push-start time. If the athletes are late in loading into the sled, the team may not have the speed or proper momentum to take the first turn correctly.

Explosive Sudden, very rapid, powerful movements as viewed during a push-start.

Fabricator A team member who is concerned with making sled or car body parts.

FIBT The Fédération Internationale de Bobsleigh et de Tobogganing is the "supreme authority" in all matters relating to international bobsled and skeleton. It makes the rules for competitions and ensures their enforcement. It also controls the World Cup, World Championships, and continental championships, as well as participation in the Olympic Games, including the confirmation of results.

Gut check A term referring to the intense pressure an athlete may feel during competition. The best athletes perform with grace under pressure.

Handling Generally refers to the performance of a sled or car while racing or practicing. How it "handles" is determined by its runners or tires, suspension geometry, and aerodynamics, among other factors.

Heats The division of a bobsled race into sections. The combined time of a team's heats (runs) determines its ranking at the event. A lower time equals a higher status.

Hit The synchronous coordination of the bobsledders' timing as they jointly move in their respective positions from a standstill to a flat-out push-start.

Hops Part of the six-item test. The athlete takes a series of five hops, with the distance jumped being measured.

House A bobsled track has a *start house* at the top of the track and a *scale house* at the bottom. The start house is where the sleds are prepared immediately prior to racing; it includes an athlete warmup area. The scale house is where each sled and its occupants are weighed at the end of the race.

Imperial system The traditional English system of measurement, now used primarily in the United States. The basic units of measurement in this system include the inch, foot, yard, and mile. The sport of bobsledding generally uses the **metric system** (see below).

Interval training A training routine in which an athlete works a series of specified exercises separated by designated rest periods or "intervals."

IOC The International Olympic Committee, which oversees the responsibilities of all Olympic Game activities.

Kreisel A 360-degree turn.

Labyrinth A three-turn combination.

Line   The best route around a track; the most efficient or quickest way around the track for a particular driver. The "high line" takes a sled or car closer to the top edge. The "low line" takes a sled or car closer to the bottom edge.

Lip   A wooden or metal safety barrier at the track's top edge to keep the sled from going off the track.

Loading   The smooth, catlike motion of the athletes as they sequentially hop, enter the sled, and assume their race positions. Loading is a key part of achieving fast push-start times.

Manual timing   Timing accomplished by hand (stopwatch) to within one-tenth of a second. Digital watches that record time to within one one-hundredth of a second are a form of manual timing, with results being rounded up to the nearest tenth (i.e., 7.58 becomes 7.6).

Metric system   An international system of measurement whose main units of length are the meter (approximately 39 inches) and centimeter (approximately 0.4 inch). All official bobsled competitions use metric measurements.

NASCAR   National Association for Stock Car Automobile Racing, an organization founded in December 1947 by William "Big Bill" France, Sr. NASCAR sanctions races, sets rules, and awards points toward championships for several types of cars using conventional (stock) parts.

Omega   A turn shaped like the Greek letter omega (Ω).

Power training   Lifting weights in a prescribed manner for the purpose of enhancing strength.

Pressure   Force applied during a push-start. Each athlete must apply a constant pressure to his or her push-handle; the force applied should be a straight linear motion that is pushed "through" the palms of each sledder's hands. The term also describes the directional intensity or G force that tells the members of a bobsled team where they are at any given time on the track, so that they know what to anticipate.

Push Sled Championships   Participation in the U.S. National Push Sled Championships in Lake Placid is a requirement for making the National Team. The USBSF selects bobsled push athletes based on the best performances in the championships. The World Push Championships are held annually in Monte Carlo, Monaco. Bobsled teams from around the world compete in shorts and T-shirts as they push a bobsled on wheels. Prince Albert Grimaldi, captain of the Monaco Bobsled Team, hosts the event.

Push-start   The start of a team's bobsled run. The athletes, from a standing start, explosively push the sled in unison up to 50 meters and then load into it.

Ragged edge Extreme. The expression "running on the ragged edge" means driving a sled or car to its extreme limits while either practicing or racing. Going "over the ragged edge" can result in loss of control.

Reasonable suspicion A term applied to the enforcement of rules governing drugs and equipment. Officials may act on "reasonable suspicion" if they have cause to believe that a driver, crew member, or other official is abusing drugs or has altered equipment in an illegal fashion. The suspect person or equipment may be required to undergo testing.

Right combination A catchall phrase used to describe why a sled (or car), team, or driver has performed well or won a race. Included are driving the right lines, good support crew, correct weight distribution, fast start, etc.

Runner friction Resistance of a bobsled's runners against the ice. Contrary to popular belief, the runners have rounded edges and are not sharp like a knife or an ice skate. A sled's runners need to glide along the ice. If they are rough, hit ruts in the ice, or cause ruts to form, friction between the sled and the ice results in slower finish times.

Sandbagger A driver who allegedly fails to drive a sled or car to its fullest potential in practice, thus being able to provide a "surprise" for his or her competitors during a race. A driver who does this is said to be *sandbagging*.

Setup The condition of a race vehicle when all current adjustments and modifications are in place.

Shotcrete Construction material used in a bobrun. Part of an artificial bobsled track consists of a double-curved surface that can only be installed by shooting the concrete in place with a high-pressure concrete pump.

Shot put An element of the six-item test, in which a metal ball (16 pounds for men, 8 pounds for women) is thrown or "pushed" for distance.

Skeleton A sliding sport in which individual athletes race headfirst, with face down and hands back, at speeds approaching 80 mph. The athlete takes a running start and loads onto a single toboggan, racing on the same tracks that bobsledders use.

Slingshot A maneuver in which the driver picks a good line going into a turn and successfully exits the turn in a clean and smooth manner. This allows the sled to pick up speed and gain precious time. A good example occurred in the first two-man race of the 1997–98 World Cup season, in Calgary, when Brian Shimer started in tenth position with a pulled hamstring and used the slingshot maneuver through the final turns of the run to gain eight positions, thereby taking the silver medal.

Sponsor An individual or business establishment that financially supports a race driver, team, race, or series of races in return for advertising and marketing benefits.

Sprints   A race at full speed for a short distance. The 30-, 60- and 100-meter sprints are part of a potential bobsledder's six-item test.

Template   A device shaped like certain vehicle parts that is used by FIBT judges or NASCAR inspectors to check the vehicle's body shape and size, to ensure that the vehicle complies with official rules.

USBSF   The United States Bobsled and Skeleton Federation. The USBSF is the nonprofit governing body for the sports of bobsled and skeleton in the United States.

USOC   The United States Olympic Committee. The USOC is responsible for representing the United States in all Olympic-sanctioned sports.

Vertical jump   The difference between an athlete's standing height and jumping height. This is part of a potential slider's six-item test.

World Championships   A single event of bobsled team heats. Run times during the event and overall World Cup ranking determine championship status.

World Cup   A series of annual bobsled races that takes place at internationally sanctioned tracks. Teams race in heats, and each team's combined run time determines ranking status.

13

Olympic and Bobsled Organizations

The organization of, and participation in, the Olympic Games requires the cooperation of a number of independent organizations.

The International Olympic Committee (IOC)

The IOC is responsible for determining where the Games will be held. It is also the obligation of its membership to uphold the principles of the Olympic Ideal and Philosophy beyond any personal, religious, national, or political interest. The IOC is responsible for sustaining the Olympic Movement.

The members of the IOC are individuals who act as the IOC's representatives in their respective countries, not as delegates of their countries within the IOC. The members meet once a year at the IOC Session. They retire at the end of the calendar year in which they turn 70 years old, unless they were elected before the opening of the 110th Session (December 11, 1999). In that case, they must retire at the age of 80. Members elected before 1966 are members for life. The IOC chooses and elects its members from among such persons as its nominations committee considers qualified. There are currently 113 members and 19 honorary members.

The International Olympic Committee's address is:
Chateau de Vidy
Case Postale 356
1007 Lausanne, Switzerland
phone: (+41) 21 621 61 11
fax: (+41) 21 621 6216
Internet: http://www.olympic.org

The National Olympic Committees

Olympic Committees have been created, with the design and objectives of the IOC, to prepare national teams to participate in the Olympic Games. Among the tasks of these committees is to promote the Olympic Movement and its principles at the national level.

The national committees work closely with the IOC in all aspects related to the Games. They are also responsible for applying the rules concerning eligibility of athletes for the Games. Today there are more than 150 national committees throughout the world.

The U.S. Olympic Committee's address is:
One Olympic Plaza
Colorado Springs, CO 80909-5760
phone: (719) 632-5551
fax: (719) 578-4654
Internet: http://www.usolympicteam.com

U.S. Bobsled Organizations

USBSF (United States Bobsled and Skeleton Federation)
Home Office
421 Old Military Rd.
P.O. Box 828
Lake Placid, NY 12946
phone: (518) 523-1842 fax: (518) 523-9491

Park City Office
Utah Olympic Park
3000 Bear Hollow Drive
Park City, UT 84060
phone: (435) 655-0220
Internet: http://www.USBSF.com
Matthew Roy, Executive Director

USBSF National Youth Development Program
Don Hass, Lake Placid Program Director
phone: (518) 523-1842
Tom Allen, Park City Program Director
phone: (435) 655-0220

Bobsled Passenger Ride Programs

ORDA (Olympic Regional Development Authority)
Lake Placid, NY 12946
phone: (518) 523-1655

Utah Olympic Park
3000 Bear Hollow Dr.
Park City, UT 84098
phone: (435) 658-4200

International Bobsled Organizations
FIBT

(Fédération Internationale de Bobsleigh et de Tobogganing)
Via Piranesi 44/b
I 20137 Milano, Italy
phone: +39.2 757-3319 fax: +39.2 738-0624
Internet: http://www.bobsleigh.com

In addition to the USBSF, the following are International Bobsleigh Associations affiliated with the FIBT. Preceding each listing is the three-letter designation for the team and sled at race time.

AHO—Netherlands Antilles

Rodel en Bob Bond
Nederlandse Antillen
Vinkelaan 2a
NL 2245 AH Wassenaar
Netherlands
phone: +31.1751 18-283   fax: +31.1751 16-606

AND—Andorra

Associatio Esportiva de Bobsleigh
Carrer Babot Camp 2, 2on, 1
Andora La Vella
phone: +33.078 20-010

ARG—Argentina

Association Argentine de Bobsleigh
Condarco, 575
1834 Temperley
phone: +54.1 292-9321   fax: +54.1 244-6599

ARM—Armenia

Armenia Bobsled, Skeleton and Luge Federation
P.O. Box 375
Newton, MA 02456 U.S.A.
phone: (617) 630-1810 fax: (617) 630-1690

ASA—American Samoa

American Samoa Bobsled Association
P.O. Box 4489
Pago Pago, American Samoa 96799
phone: (684) 633-5058 fax: (684) 633-5059

AUS—Australia

Australian National Bobsleigh Association, Inc.
P.O. Box 410
Burnside, South Australia 5066
phone: +61.8 364-4911 fax: +61.8 364-4990

AUT—Austria

Osterreichischer Bob und Skeletonverband
Landessportheim
Olympia-StraBe, 10a
A 6020 Innsbruck
phone: +43.512 341-329 fax: +43.512 348-152

BEL—Belgium

Federation Belge de Bobsleigh et de Luge
Stentjeslaan, 11
B 2550 Kontich—Antwerpen
phone: +32.3 458-2183 fax: +32.3 458-2183

BIH—Bosnia-Herzegovina

Bob Association of Bosnia and Herzegovina
Kranjcevica, 13
71000 Sarajevo
phone: +387.71 442-166   fax: +387.71 440-956

BRA—Brazil

Brazilian Bobsled, Skeleton and Luge Association
P.O. Box 435
Norwell, MA 02061
phone: (781) 659-3367   fax: (781) 659-7363

BUL—Bulgaria

Bulgarischer Verband fur Bobsleigh und Tobogganing
Levski Street No. 75
BG 1000 Sofia
phone: +359.2 865-267   fax: +359.2 879-670

CAN—Canada

Bobsleigh and Skeleton Canada
88 Canada Olympic Road SW
Calgary, AB, T3B 5R CANADA
phone: (613) 748-5610   fax: (613) 748-5773

CHI—Chile

Bob and Skeleton Club Condor
Schloss-Strasse, 8
CH-4133 Pratteln, Switzerland
phone: +41.61 821-3285   fax: +41.61 821-3285

CHN—People's Republic of China

Chinese Bobsleigh and Tobogganing Association
9 Tiyuguan Road, Beijing
phone: 750-971   fax: 22323 CHOC CN

CZE—Czech Republic

Cesky Svaz Boby a Skeleton
Mezi Stadiony, Post. Schr. 40
CR 160 17 PRAHA 6
Tel : +42.2 356-926   fax: +420.2 356-926

DEN— Denmark

Bobslaeddeklubben Danmark
Rebekkavej, 38, 2.TV
DK 2900 HELLERUP
phone: +45.39 404-743   fax: +45.39 404-743

ESP—Spain

Federación Española Deportes de Invierno Comité de
Bobsleigh
Infanta Maria Teresa 14
E 28016 Madrid
phone: +34.1 344-0944   fax: +34.1 344-1826

FIN—Finland

Finnish Bob and Skeleton Federation
Daniel Hjort st 6
SF 20880 Turku
phone: +358.21 469-2670   fax: +358.21 469-2671

FRA—France

Fédération Française des Sports de Glace
35 rue Félicien David
F 75016 Paris France
phone: +33.6 7215-6210   fax: +33.494 853-105

GBR—Great Britain

British Bobsleigh Association
Albany House
5 New Street
SALISBURY, Warminster
Wiltshire, SP1 2PH U.K.
phone: +44.1722 340-014

GER—Germany

Deutcher Bob und Schlittensportverband
An der Schießstatte, 6
D 83471 Berchtesgaden
phone: +49.8652 9588-0   fax: +49.8652 9588-22

GRE—Greece

Hellenic Ice Sports Federation
272 B, Bl. Venizelou (Thiseos) Kalithea
17675 Athens
phone: +30.1 684-9324   fax: +30.1 685-8281

HOL—Netherlands

Bob en Slee Bond Nederland
P.O.Box 11127
2301 EC Leiden
The Netherlands
phone: +31 (0) 6.53819495   fax: +31 (0) 71.5665424

HUN—Hungary

Hungarian Skating Federation
Bobsleigh Section
Dozsa György ut 1-3
1143 Budapest
phone: +36.1 252-2369   fax: +36.1 252-2369

IRL—Ireland

Irish Bobsleigh and Luge Association
Maycrest, Navan Road
Blanchardstown, Dublin, 15
phone: +353.1 821-3275   fax: +353.1 821-3275

ISV—Virgin Islands

USA Virgin Islands Bobsled Federation
6501 Red Hook Plaza, Suite 61
St. Thomas, USVI 00802
phone: (809) 775-9442   fax: (809) 775-9438

ITA—Italy

Federazione Italiana Sport Invernali Sezione Bob
Via Piranesi, 44/B
I 20137 Milano Italy
phone: +39.2 757-3319   fax: +39.2 738-0624

JAM—Jamaica

Jamaica Bobsled Federation
9 Forest Glen
Forest Gardens, Kingston 19
phone: (809) 931-7845

JPN—Japan

Japan Bobsleigh and Luge Federation
524 Agata-Machi
Nagano City 380-8524
phone: +81.26 235-6260   fax: +81.26 235-6261

KAZ—Kazakhstan

Bobsleigh Federation of the Republic of Kazakhatan
Gorky Park, "Spartak Stadium"
480023 Alma-Ata
phone: +7.3272 304-857   fax: +7.3272 631-207

LAT—Latvia

Latvia Bobsled Federation
Kuldigas, 39
Riga, LV 1083
phone: +371.7 601-926   fax: +371.7 601-922

LIE—Liechtenstein

Bob and Skeleton Club Liechtenstein
Aeulestraße, 74
Postfach 461, FL9494 SCHAAN
phone: +41.75 371-1168   fax: +41.75 371-1168

MEX—Mexico

Mexican Bobsled Team
Barcelona 2235 - Sta Monica
Guadalajara, Jalisco C.P. 44220
phone: +52.3 660-9502   fax: +52.3 660-9502

MON—Monaco

Federation Monegasque de Bobsleigh and de Skeleton
2 Avenue des Castellands
MC 98000 Monaco, Fontville
phone: +377.93 104-060   fax: +377.93 507-014

NOR—Norway

Norges Ake-og Bobforbund
Serviceboks 1, Ulleval Stadion
Sognsveien, 75 L
N0840 OSLO
phone: +47.21 029000   fax: +47.21 029003

NZL—New Zealand

New Zealand Bobsleigh and Skeleton Association
P.O. Box 781
Blenheim New Zealand
phone: +64.3 577-8722

POL—Poland

Polski Zwiazek Sportow Saneczkowych
UI. Marymoncka, 34
PL 01-813 Warszawa
phone: +48.22 347-942

POR—Portugal

Bobsleigh Clube de Portugal
187 Lord Seaton Road
Willowdale, Ontario M2P 1L1 Canada
phone: (416) 512-8706

PUR—Puerto Rico

Bobsleigh Puerto Rico
501 Calle Cerra no. 8F
San Juan, Puerto Rico 00907
phone: (809) 725-0892   fax: (809) 725-0892

ROM—Romania

Federatia Romana de Bob
Strada Vasile Conta, 16
R 70139 Bucuresti
phone: +40.1 211-5550/209   fax: + 40.1 210-6521

RSA—South Africa

Cape Town Bobsleigh Club
Grannenweg, 20
D 50933 KÖLN, Germany
phone: +49.221 947-3071   fax: +49.221 947-3072

RUS—Russia

All-Russian Bobsleigh Federation
Luzhnetskaja nab. 8
119270 Moskva
phone: +7.095 201-0911   fax: +7.095 248-0814

SAM—Samoa

Western Samoa Bobsleigh and Skeleton Association
22 Eaton Road, Hillsborough
Auckland 4, New Zealand
phone: +64.9 375-8999   fax: +64.9 375-8877

SMR—San Marino

Federazione Sanmarinese Sport Invernali
Via XXV Marzo, 11
47031 Domagnano
phone: +39.549 902-706   fax: +39.549 902-516

SUI—Switzerland

Schweizerischer Bobsleigh, Schlittel und
Skeletonsportverband
Postfach 9
CH 8032 Zurich, Switzerland
phone: +41.1 397-1097   fax: +41.1 397-1098

SWE—Sweden

Svenska Bob och Rodelforbundet
Box 102
SE-12122 Johanneshov, Sweden
phone: +46.8 722-4010   fax: +46.8 5504-9185

TPE—Chinese Taipei

Amateur Bobsleigh and Luge Association
Room 604, No. 20 Chu Lun Street
Taipei, Taiwan, Formosa
phone: +886.2 775-8728   fax: +886.2 778-2473

TRI—Trinidad and Tobago

Trinadad and Tobago Bobsleigh Federation
P.O. Box 3863
Moscow, Idaho 83843 U.S.A.
phone: (208) 882-1585   fax: (208) 885-8937

UKR—Ukraine

Bobsleigh Federation of Ukraine
No. 1 Tupolev Street
252062 Kiev
phone: +380.44 444-2424   fax: +380.44 449-9996

VEN—Venezuela

Association Venezolana de Bob, Trineo y Skeleton
Avenida Urdaneta, Esq. Veroes
Ed. America, Piso 7, Of. 706
Caracas, Venezuela

14

World Champions

World Bobsleigh Two and Four Man
Championship Medal Winners (including Olympic
Winter Games)

1958 Garmisch-Partenkirchen, FRG

1st   Eugenio Monti, Renzo Alvera (ITA)
2nd Sergio Zardini, Sergio Siorpaes (ITA)
3rd   Paul Aste, Heinz Isser (AUT)
1st   Hans Roesch, Alfred Hammer, Theo Bauer, Walter Haller (FRG)
2nd Franz Schelle, Eduard Kaltenberger, Josef Sterff, Otto Goebl (FRG)
3rd   Sergio Zardini, M. Bogana, Renato Mocellini, Alberto Righini (ITA)

1959 St. Moritz, SUI

1st   Eugenio Monti, Renzo Alvera (ITA)
2nd Sergio Zardini, Luciano Alberti (ITA)
3rd   Arthur Tyler, Charles Thomas Butler (USA)
1st   Arthur Tyler, Garry Sheffield, Parker Vooris, Charles Thomas Butler (USA)
2nd Sergio Zardini, Alberto Righini, Ferruccio Della Torre, Romano Bonagura (ITA)
3rd   Franz Schelle, Hartl Geiger, Josef Sterff, Otto Goebl (FRG)

1960 Cortina d'Ampezzo, ITA (not Olympics)

1st   Eugenio Monti, Renzo Alvera (ITA)
2nd   Franz Schelle, Otto Goebl (FRG)
3rd   Sergio Zardini, Luciano Alberti (ITA)
1st   Eugenio Monti, Furio Nordio, Sergio Siorpaes, Renzo Alvera (ITA)
2nd   Hans Roesch, Alfred Hammer, Albert Kandlbinder, Theo Bauer (FRG)
3rd   Max Angst, Hansjörg Hirschbuhl, Göpf Kottmann, René Kuhl (SUI)

1961 Lake Placid, USA

1st   Eugenio Monti, Sergio Siorpaes (ITA)
2nd   Garry Sheffield, Jerry Tennant (USA)
3rd   Sergio Zardini, Romano Bonagura (ITA)
1st   Eugenio Monti, Furio Nordio, Benito Rigoni, Sergio Siorpaes (ITA)
2nd   Stanley Benham, Garry Sheffield, Jerry Tennant, Chuck Pandolph (USA)
3rd   Gunnar Ahs, Gunnar Carpö, Erik Wennerberg, Börje Bengt Hedblom (SWE)

1962 Garmisch-Partenkirchen, FRG

1st   Rinaldo Ruatti, Enrico De Lorenzo (ITA)
2nd   Sergio Zardini, Romano Bonagura (ITA)
3rd   Hans Maurer, Adolf Wörmann (FRG)
1st   Franz Schelle, Josef Sterff, Ludwig Siebert, Otto Goebl (FRG)
2nd   Sergio Zardini, Ferruccio Della Torre, Enrico de Lorenzo, Romano Bonagura (ITA)
3rd   Franz lsser, Pepi lsser, Heini lsser, Fritz Isser (AUT)

1963 Igls, AUT

1st   Eugenio Monti, Sergio Siorpaes (ITA)
2nd   Sergio Zardini, Romano Bonagura (ITA)
3rd   Anthony Nash, Robin Dixon (GBR)
1st   Sergio Zardini, Ferruccio Della Torre, Renato Mocellini, Romano Bonagura (ITA)
2nd   Angelo Frigerio, Mario Pallua, Luigi de Bettin, Sergio Mocellini (ITA)
3rd   Erwin Thaler, Reinhold Durnthaler, Josef Nairz, Adolf Koxeder (AUT)

1964 Igls, AUT (Olympics)

1st   Anthony Nash, Robin Dixon (GBR)
2nd   Sergio Zardini, Romano Bonagura (ITA)
3rd   Eugenio Monti, Sergio Siorpaes (ITA)
1st   Victor Emery, Douglas Anakin, John Emery, Peter Kirby (CAN)
2nd   Erwin Thaler, Josef Nairz, Reinhold Durnthaler, Adolf Koxeder (AUT)
3rd   Eugenio Monti, Benito Rigoni, Gildo Siorpaes, Sergio Siorpaes (ITA)

1965 St. Moritz, SUI

1st   Anthony Nash, Robin Dixon (GBR)
2nd   Rinaldo Ruatti, Enrico De Lorenzo (ITA)
3rd   Victor Emery, Mike Young (CAN)
1st   Victor Emery, Gerald Presley, Mike Young, Peter Kirby (CAN)
2nd   Nevio de Zordo, ltalo de Lorenzo, Pietro Lesana, Roberto Mocellini (ITA)
3rd   Fred Fortune, Richard Knuckles, Joe Wilson, James Lord (USA)

1966 Cortina d'Ampezzo, ITA

1st` Eugenio Monti, Sergio Siorpaes (ITA)
2nd Gianfranco Gaspari, Leonardo Cavallini (ITA)
3rd Anthony Nash, Robin Dixon (GBR)
Four-man race abandoned after Toni Pensperger's fatal crash;
gold medal given posthumously to Pensberger, Ludwig Siebert,
Helmut Wurzer, Roland Ebert (FRG)

1967 Alpe d'Huez, FRA

1st Erwin Thaler, Reinhold Durnthaler (AUT)
2nd Nevio De Zordo, Edoardo Tinter de Martin (ITA)
3rd Howard Clifton, James Crall (USA)

1968 Alpe d'Huez, Grenoble, FRA (Olympics)

1st Eugenio Monti, Luciano De Paolis (ITA)
2nd Horst Floth, Pepi Bader (FRG)
3rd Ion Panturu, Nicolae Neagoe (ROM)
1st Eugenio Monti, Roberto Zandonella, Mario Armano,
Luciano De Paolis (ITA)
2nd Erwin Thaler, Herbert Gruber, Josef Eder, Reinhold
Durnthaler (AUT)
3rd Jean Wicki, Hans Candrian, Willi Hofmann, Walter Graf
(SUI)

1969 Lake Placid, USA

1st Nevio De Zordo, Adriano Frassinelli (ITA)
2nd Ion Panturu, Dumitru Focseneanu (ROM)
3rd Gianfranco Gaspari, Mario Armano (ITA)
1st Wolfgang Zimmerer, Stefan Gaisreiter, Walter Steinbauer,
Peter Utzschneider (FRG)
2nd Gianfranco Gaspari, Sergio Pompanin, Roberto Zandonella,
Mario Armano (ITA)
3rd Les Fenner, Robert William Huscher, Howard Siler, Allen
Hachigian (USA)

1970 St. Moritz, SUI

1st Horst Floth, Pepi Bader (FRG)
2nd Wolfgang Zimmerer, Peter Utzschneider (FRG)
3rd Gion Caviezel, Hans Candrian (SUI)
1st Nevio De Zordo, Roberto Zandonella, Mario Armano, Luciano De Paolis (ITA)
2nd Wolfgang Zimmerer, Walter Steinbauer, Pepi Bader, Peter Utzschneider (FRG)
3rd René Stadler, Hans Candrian, Max Forster, Peter Schärer (SUI)

1971 Cervinia, ITA

1st Gianfranco Gaspari, Mario Armano (ITA)
2nd Enzo Vicario, Corrado Dal Fabbro (ITA)
3rd Herbert Gruber, Josef Oberhauser (AUT)
1st René Stadler, Max Forster, Erich Schärer, Peter Schärer (SUI)
2nd Oscar d'Andrea, Alessandro Bignozzi, Antonio Brabcaccio, Renzo Caldara (ITA)
3rd Wolfgang Zimmerer, Stefan Gaisreiter, Walter Steinbauer, Peter Utzschneider (FRG)

1972 Sapporo, Mount Teine, JPN (Olympics)

1st Wolfgang Zimmerer, Peter Utzschneider (FRG)
2nd Horst Floth, Pepi Bader (FRG)
3rd Jean Wicki, Edi Hubacher (SUI)
1st Jean Wicki, Hans Leutenegger, Werner Camichel, Edy Hubacher (SUI)
2nd Nevio De Zordo, Adriano Frassinelli, Corrado Dal Fabbro, Gianni Bonichon (ITA)
3rd Wolfgang Zimmerer, Stefan Gaisreiter, Walter Steinbauer, Peter Utzschneider (FRG)

1973 Lake Placid, USA

1st Wolfgang Zimmerer, Peter Utzschneider (FRG)
2nd Hans Candrian, Heinz Schenker (SUI)
3rd Ion Panturu, Dumitru Focseneanu (ROM)
1st René Stadler, Werner Camichel, Erich Schärer, Peter Schärer (SUI)
2nd Werner Delle Karth, Walter Delle Karth, Hans Eichinger, Fritz Sperling (AUT)
3rd Wolfgang Zimmerer, Stefan Gaisreiter, Walter Steinbauer, Peter Utzschneider (FRG)

1974 St. Moritz, SUI

1st Wolfgang Zimmerer, Peter Utzschneider (FRG)
2nd Georg Heibl, Fritz Ohlwärter (FRG)
3rd Fritz Lüdi, Karl Häseli (SUI)
1st Wolfgang Zimmerer, Albert Wurzer, Peter Utzschneider, Manfred Schumann (FRG)
2nd Hans Candrian, Guido Casty, Yves Marchand, Gaudenz Beeli (SUI)
3rd Werner Delle Karth, Hans Eichinger, Walter Delle Karth, Fritz Sperling (AUT)

1975 Cervinia, ITA

1st Giorgio Alvera, Franco Perruquet (ITA)
2nd Georg Heibl, Fritz Ohlwärter (FRG)
3rd Fritz Lüdi, Karl Häseli (SUI)
1st Erich Schärer, Werner Camichel, Josef Benz, Peter Schärer (SUI)
2nd Wolfgang Zimmerer, Peter Utzschneider, Albert Wurzer, Fritz Ohlwärter (FRG)
3rd Manfred Stengl, Gert Krenn, Franz Jakob, Armin Vilas (AUT)

1976 Igls, AUT (Olympics)

1st   Meinhard Nehmer, Bernhard Germeshausen (GDR)
2nd   Wolfgang Zimmerer, Manfred Schumann (FRG)
3rd   Erich Schärer, Josef Benz (SUI)
1st   Meinhard Nehmer, Jochen Babock, Bernhard Germeshausen, Bernhard Lehmann (GDR)
2nd   Erich Schärer, Ulrich Bächli, Rudolf Marti, Josef Benz (SUI)
3rd   Wolfgang Zimmerer, Peter Utzschneider, Bodo Bittner, Manfred Schumann (FRG)

1977 St. Moritz, SUI

1st   Hans Hiltebrand, Heinz Meier (SUI)
2nd   Fritz Lüdi, Hansjörg Trachsel (SUI)
3rd   Stefan Gaisreiter, Manfred Schumann (FRG)
1st   Meinhard Nehmer, Hans-Jürgen Gerhardt, Bernhard Germeshausen, Raimund Bethge (GDR)
2nd   Erich Schärer, Ulrich Bächli, Rudolf Marti, Josef Benz (SUI)
3rd   Jakob Resch, Herbert Berg, Fritz Ohlwärter, Walter Barfuss (FRG)

1978 Lake Placid, USA

1st   Erich Schärer, Josef Benz (SUI)
2nd   Meinhard Nehmer, Raimund Bethge (GDR)
3rd   Jakob Resch, Walter Barfuss (FRG)
1st   Horst Schönau, Horst Bernhardt, Bogdan Musiol, Harald Seifert (GDR)
2nd   Erich Schärer, Ulrich Bächli, Rudolf Marti, Josef Benz (SUI)
3rd   Meinhard Nehmer, Raimund Bethge, Bernhard Germeshausen, Hans-Jürgen Gerhardt (GDR)

1979 Königssee, FRG

1st Erich Schärer, Josef Benz (SUI)
2nd Stefan Gaisreiter, Manfred Schumann, Fritz Ohlwärter
    (4th heat because Schumann was injured (FRG)
3rd Toni Mangold, Stefan Späte (FRG)
1st Stefan Gaisreiter, Hans Wagner, Heinz Busche, Dieter
    Gebhard (FRG)
2nd Meinhard Nehmer, Detlef Richter, Bernhard
    Germeshausen, Hans-Jürgen Gerhardt (GDR)
3rd Erich Schärer, Ulrich Bächli, Hansjörg Trachsel, Josef Benz
    (SUI)

1980 Lake Placid, USA (Olympics)

1st Erich Schärer, Josef Benz (SUI)
2nd Bernhard Germeshausen, Hans-Jürgen Gerhardt (GDR)
3rd Meinhard Nehmer, Bogdan Musiol (GDR)
1st Meinhard Nehmer, Bogdan Musiol, Bernhard
    Germeshausen, Hans-Jürgen Gerhardt (GDR)
2nd Erich Schärer, Ulrich Bächli, Rudolf Marti, Josef Benz (SUI)
3rd Horst Schönau, Roland Wetzig, Detlef Richter, Andreas
    Kirchner (GDR)

1981 Cortina d'Ampezzo, ITA

1st Bernhard Germeshausen, Hans-Jürgen Gerhardt (GDR)
2nd Horst Schönau, Andreas Kirchner (GDR)
3rd Erich Schärer, Josef Benz (SUI)
1st Bernhard Germeshausen, Henry Gerlach, Michael Trübner,
    Hans-Jürgen Gerhardt (GDR)
2nd Hans Hiltebrand, Kurt Poletti, Franz Weinberger, Franz
    Isenegger (SUI)
3rd Erich Schärer, Max Rüegg, Tony Rüegg, Josef Benz (SUI)

1982 St. Moritz, SUI

1st   Erich Schärer, Max Rüegg (SUI)
2nd Hans Hiltebrand, Ulrich Bächli (SUI)
3rd   Horst Schönau, Andreas Kirchner (GDR)
1st   Silvio Giobellina, Heinz Stettler, Urs Salzmann, Rico Freiermuth (SUI)
2nd Bernhard Lehmann, Roland Wetzig, Bogdan Musiol, Eberhard Weise (GDR)
3rd   Erich Schärer, Franz lsenegger, Tony Rüegg, Max Rüegg (SUI)

1983 Lake Placid, USA

1st   Ralph Pichler, Urs Leuthold (SUI)
2nd Erich Schärer, Max Rüegg (SUI)
3rd   Wolfgang Hoppe, Dietmar Schauerhammer (GDR)
1st   Ekkehard Fasser, Kurt Poletti, Hans Märchy, Rolf Strittmatter (SUI)
2nd Klaus Kopp, Gerhard Öchsle, Günther Neuburger, Hajo Schumacher (FRG)
3rd   Detlef Richter, Henry Gerlach, Thomas Forch, Dietmar Jerke (GDR)

1984 Sarajevo, YUG (Olympics)

1st   Wolfgang Hoppe, Dietmar Schauerhammer (GDR)
2nd Bernhard Lehmann, Bogdan Musiol (GDR)
3rd   Sintis Ekmanis, Vladimir Alexandrov (URS)
1st   Wolfgang Hoppe, Roland Wetzig, Dietmar Schauerhammer, Andreas Kirchner (GDR)
2nd Bernhard Lehmann, Bogdan Musiol, lngo Voge, Eberhard Weise (GDR)
3rd   Silvio Giobellina, Heinz Stettler, Urs Salzmann, Rico Freiermuth (SUI)

1985 Cervinia, ITA

1st Wolfgang Hoppe, Dietmar Schauerhammer (GDR)
2nd Detlef Richter, Steffen Grummt (GDR)
3rd Sintis Ekmanis, Nikolai Schirov (URS)
1st Bernhard Lehmann, Matthias Trübner, lngo Voge, Steffen Grummt (GDR)
2nd Detlef Richter, Dietmar Jerke, Bodo Ferl, Matthias Legler (GDR)
3rd Silvio Giobellina, Heinz Stettler, Urs Salzmann, Rico Freiermuth (SUI)

1986 Königssee, FRG

1st Wolfgang Hoppe, Dietmar Schauerhammer (GDR)
2nd Ralph Pichler, Celest Poltera (SUI)
3rd Detlef Richter, Steffen Grummt (GDR)
1st Erich Schärer, Kurt Meier, Erwin Fassbind, André Kiser (SUI)
2nd Peter Kienast, Franz Siegl, Gerhard RedI, Christian Mark (AUT)
3rd Ralph Pichler, Heinrich Notter, Celest Poltera, Roland Beerli (SUI)

1987 St. Moritz, SUI

1st Ralph Pichler, Celest Poltera (SUI)
2nd Hans Hiltebrand, André Kiser (SUI)
3rd Wolfgang Hoppe, Dietmar Schauerhammer (GDR)
1st Hans Hiltebrand, Urs Fehlmann, Erwin Fassbind, André Kiser (SUI)
2nd Wolfgang Hoppe, Bogdan Musiol, Roland Wetzig, Dietmar Schauerhammer (GDR)
3rd Ralph Pichler, Heinrich Ott, Edgar Dietsche, Celest Poltera (SUI)

1988 Calgary, CAN (Olympics)

1st   Janis Kipurs, Vladimir Kozlov (URS)
2nd   Wolfgang Hoppe, Bogdan Musiol (GDR)
3rd   Bernhard Lehmann, Mario Hoyer (GDR)
1st   Ekkehard Fasser, Kurt Meier, Marcel Fässler, Werner Stocker (SUI)
2nd   Wolfgang Hoppe, Dietmar Schauerhammer, Bogdan Musiol, lngo Voge (GDR)
3rd   Janis Kipurs, Guntis Ossis, Juris Tone, Vladimir Kozlov (URS)

1989 Cortina d'Ampezzo, ITA

1st   Wolfgang Hoppe, Bogdan Musiol (GDR)
2nd   Gustav Weder, Bruno Gerber (SUI)
3rd   Janis Kipurs, Aldis lntlers (URS)
1st   Gustav Weder, Bruno Gerber, Lorenz Schindelholz, Curdin Morell (SUI)
2nd   Nico Baracchi, Christian Reich, Donat Acklin, René Mangold (SUI)
3rd   Wolfgang Hoppe, Bodo Ferl, Bogdan Musiol, lngo Voge (GDR)

1990 St. Moritz, SUI (Bobsleigh Centenary)

1st   Gustav Weder, Bruno Gerber (SUI)
2nd   Harald Czudaj, Axel Jang (GDR)
3rd   Wolfgang Hoppe, Bogdan Musiol (GDR)
1st   Gustav Weder, Bruno Gerber, Lorenz Schindelholz, Curdin Morell (SUI)
2nd   Harald Czudaj, Tino Bonk, Alexander Szelig, Axel Jang (GDR)
3rd   Ingo Appelt, Gerhard Redl, Jürgen Mandl, Harald Winkler (AUT)

1991 Altenberg, GER

1st Rudi Lochner, Markus Zimmermann (GER)
2nd Gustav Weder, Curdin Morell (SUI)
3rd Wolfgang Hoppe, René Hannemann (GER)
1st Wolfgang Hoppe, Bogdan Musiol, Axel Kühn, Christoph Langen (GER)
2nd Gustav Weder, Bruno Gerber, Lorenz Schindelholz, Curdin Morell (SUI)
3rd Harald Czudaj, Tino Bonk, Axel Jang, Alexander Szelig (GER)

1992 Albertville, La Plagne, FRA (Olympics)

1st Gustav Weder, Donat Acklin (SUI)
2nd Rudi Lochner, Markus Zimmermann (GER)
3rd Christoph Langen, Günther Eger (GER)
1st Ingo Appelt, Harald Winkler, Gerhard Haidacher, Thomas Schroll (AUT)
2nd Wolfgang Hoppe, Bogdan Musiol, Axel Kühn, René Hannemann (GER)
3rd Gustav Weder, Donat Acklin, Lorenz Schindelholz, Curdin Morell (SUI)

1993 Igls, AUT

1st Christoph Langen, Peer Joechel (GER)
2nd Gustav Weder, Donat Acklin (SUI)
3rd Wolfgang Hoppe, René Hannemann (GER)
1st Gustav Weder, Donat Acklin, Kurt Meier, Domenico Semeraro (SUI)
2nd Hubert Schösser, Harald Winkler, Gerhard Redl, Gerhard Haidacher (AUT)
3rd Brian Shimer, Bryan Leturgez, Karlos Kirby, Randy Jones (USA)

1994 Lillehammer, NOR (Olympics)

1st   Gustav Weder, Donat Acklin (SUI)
2nd   Reto Götschi, Guido Acklin (SUI)
3rd   Günther Huber, Stefano Ticci (ITA)
1st   Harald Czudaj, Karsten Brannasch, Olaf Hampel, Alexander Szelig (GER)
2nd   Gastac Weder, Donat Acklin, Kurt Meier, Domenico Semeraro (SUI)
3rd   Wolfgang Hoppe, Ulf Hielscher, René Hannemann, Carsten Embach (GER)

1995 Winterberg, GER

1st   Christoph Langen, Olaf Hampel (GER)
2nd   Pierre Lueders, Jack Pyc (CAN)
3rd   Eric Alard, Eric Le Chanony (FRA)
1st   Wolfgang Hoppe, René Hannemann, Ulf Hielscher, Carsten Embach (GER)
2nd   Hubert Schösser, Gerhard Redl, Thomas Schroll, Martin Schützenauer (AUT)
3rd   Harald Czudaj, Thorsten Voss, Udo Lehmann, Alexander Szelig (GER)

1996 Calgary, CAN

1st   Christoph Langen, Markus Zimmermann (GER)
2nd   Pierre Lueders, Dave MacEachern (CAN
3rd   Reto Götschi, Guido Acklin (SUI
1st   Christoph Langen, Markus Zimmermann, Sven Rühr, Olaf Hampel (GER)
2nd   Marcel Rohner, Markus Wasser, Thomas Schreiber, Roland Tanner (SUI)
3rd   Wolfgang Hoppe, Torsten Voss, Sven Peter, Carsten Embach (GER)

1997 St. Moritz, SUI

1st   Reto Götschi, Guido Acklin (SUI)
2nd Günther Huber, Antonio Tartaglia (ITA)
3rd Brian Shimer, Robert Olesen (USA)
1st   Wolfgang Hoppe, Sven Rühr, René Hannemann, Carsten Embach (GER)
2nd Dirk Wiese, Christoph Bartsch, Torsten Voss, Michael Liekmeier (GER)
3rd Brian Shimer, Chip Minton, Randy Jones, Robert Olesen (USA)

1998 Nagano, JPN (Olympics)

1st   Günther Huber, Antonio Tartaglia (ITA) Pierre Lueders, Dave MacEachern (CAN)
3rd Christoph Langen, Markus Zimmermann (GER)
1st   Christoph Langen, Markus Zimmerman, Marco Jacobs, Olaf Hampel (GER)
2nd Marcel Rohner, Markus Nüssli, Markus Wasser, Beat Seitz (SUI)
3rd Sean Olsson, Dean Ward, Courtney Rumbolt, Paul Attwood (GBR)

1999 Cortina d'Ampezzo, ITA

1st   Günther Huber, Enrico Costa, Ubaldo Ranzi (ITA) - Costa was injured in 1st heat
2nd   Christoph Langen, Markus Zimmermann (GER)
3rd Bruno Mingeon, Emmanuel Hostache (FRAU)
1st   Bruno Mingeon, Emmanuel Hostache, Eric Le Chanony, Max Robert (FRA)
2nd Marcel Rohner, Markus Nüssli, Beat Hefti, Silvio Schaufelberger (SUI)
3rd Pierre Lueders, Ken Leblanc, Ben Hindle, Matt Hindle (CAN)

2000 Altenberg, GER

1st   Christoph Langen, Markus Zimmermann (GER)
2nd   André Lange, Rene Hoppe (GER)
3rd   Christian Reich, Urs Aeberhard (SUI)
1st   André Lange, Rene Hoppe, Lars Behrendt, Carsten Embach
     · (GER)
2nd   Christoph Langen, Markus Zimmermann, Tomas Plazter,
     Sven Rühr (GER)
3rd   Christian Reich, Bruno Aeberhard, Urs Aeberhand,
     Domenic Keller (SUI)

2001 St. Moritz, SUI

1st   Christoph Langen, Marco Jakobs (GER)
2nd   Reto Götschi, Cedric Grand (SUI)
3rd   Martin Annen, Beat Hefti (SUI)
1st   Christoph Langen, Markus Zimmermann, Sven Peter, Alex
     Metzger (GER)
2nd   Andre Lange, Lars Behrendt, Rene Hoppe, Carsten
     Embach(GER)
3rd   Christian Reich, Steve Anderhub, Urs Aeberhard, Dominic
     Keller (SUI)

Women's Bobsleigh World Championship

2001 Calgary, CAN

1st   Francoise Burdet, Katharina Sutter (SUI)
2nd   Jean Racine, Jennifer Davidson (USA)
3rd   Susi Erdmann, Tanja Hees (GER)